The Motivation MESSAGE And MEANING Behind The Music

I can do all things through Christ which strengtheneth me.
(Philippians 4:13)

The Motivation MESSAGE And MEANING Behind The Music

I can do all things through Christ which strengtheneth me.
(Philippians 4:13)

By
MARANDA FORNEY

Chicago, Illinois
U.S.A.

THE MOTIVATION, MESSAGE AND MEANING BEHIND
THE MUSIC
Copyright © 2004 by Maranda Forney
All rights reserved.
Printed in the United States of America.
ISBN 0-9752960-0-0

Published by:
Forney Publishing
P.O. Box 806394
Chicago, Illinois 60680-6394

Content Consultant: Pastor Keith Cistrunk
Editors: Michael Forney, George Watkins and Charm Watkins
Cover: Maranda Forney

This book or parts thereof may not be reproduced in any form without written permission from the publisher. Without written consent from the author, any reproduction of this book or parts thereof is unlawful according to the 1976 United States Copyright Act.

Unless otherwise indicated, all Scripture references are from the King James Version of the Bible.

Unless otherwise indicated, all definitions are from *The American Heritage Dictionary Second Edition.* Boston, Massachusetts: Houghton Mifflin Company, 1982.

Dedication

I thank and dedicate this project to God my Father for His gifts, wisdom, and guidance. It is He who has given me the desires of my heart and the wisdom and strength to accomplish my goals. His Word is a lamp unto my feet and a light unto my pathway and without Him this project would not exist.

To my best friend, partner and husband, Michael Forney for your consistent encouragement and emotional support. I love you so much!

To George J. Watkins Jr. for always demanding nothing but the best from me. I may not have appreciated it as a child but I am very grateful as an adult. I love you daddy! Charm Watkins, my beautiful mother, thank you for always believing in me. You are truly an inspiration and I love you very much!

To my grandparents, Mom & Pop Golden, thank you for your wisdom, I love you!

To my sister Robin Watkins for your administrative support and research. I love you! Melissa Forney, my sister-in-law who continued to press upon Michael and I to visit her church and as a result we were born again! Our lives have never been the same! I love you!

Finally, to my seven beautiful children: Charm, Tatianna, Michael, Timothy, Benjamin,

Joseph and Amirah. I hope that you all are encouraged and inspired to fulfill your Godly destiny as you have watched me pursue mine. You have been my motivation and inspiration. I love you!!!

Acknowledgments

I would like to acknowledge Pastors Gregory and Grace Dickow of Life Changers International Church for your sound teaching of the Word of God. Pastor Keith and Dana Cistrunk, for not only the encouragement but also all the support and assistance that you so willingly contributed to make sure this project was completed. Doug and Lisa Thiel, Lisa and Darius King, and Mary and Emanuel Thomas III.

Bishop Brian Keith and Prophetess Donna Williams for not only leading me to the Lord but for the prophetic, radical, and passionate teaching.

The late Pastor Gregory Tolliver and his wife Pastor Yolanda Tolliver. Pastor Tolliver it was you who first encouraged me to pursue my music after my rebirth. Thank you so very much for believing in me!!!

Valerie and Greg Landfair, I thank God everyday for you. You two are so very special that words cannot express how much I esteem and appreciate you both. I pray that God continue to RICHLY bless you. Greg I agree with Pastor Bynum, I too hope that you can bring your guitar to heaven. Pastor Tom Bynum and his beautiful wife Samantha, it was an honor to be a part of your ministry.

Bishop Bernard Jordan and Prophetess Debra Jordan of Zoe Ministries, thank you for your

Acknowledgments

many prophetic words of wisdom. Evangelist Glenda "Kay" Freeman, a great woman and prophet of God who has encouraged me since my spiritual rebirth.

    Thank you to all the background vocalists and musicians.

THE MOTIVATION, MESSAGE AND MEANING BEHIND THE MUSIC

The Vision

And the Lord answered me, and said, Write the vision, and make it plain upon tables, that he may run that readeth it." (Habakkuk 2:2)

In September of 1991, I received Jesus Christ as my personal Lord and Savior. For over twelve years I have been in the Presence of the Lord where I have heard the voice, known the thoughts and felt the heartbeat of God. However, it was not until November of 2003 that I received the revelation of being "in His presence."

In the beginning God created Adam and Eve. God told Adam not to eat of the tree of knowledge of good and evil in the Garden of Eden, otherwise he would die. Adam and Eve were disobedient, ate from the tree, and not only lost their sense of holiness but were removed from the presence of God.

Without the presence of God, man could no longer have a personal relationship with God. Therefore, God the Father had to send one that was greater, His Son, Jesus Christ to redeem us from sin. When Jesus Christ died on the cross, sin died with Him and when He rose from the dead and ascended into heaven to be with the Father, His presence was restored in the earth. As a result, when we confess with our mouths and believe in our hearts that God raised His Son, Jesus Christ from the dead, we are saved. The presence of God dwells within us and we in Him.

My vision is to let the people of God know that we can not sing, dance or preach our way "into His presence." Because of the blood of the Lamb, by faith we abide in God and He in us. All we have to do is rest in His presence and we will experience power, riches, wisdom, strength, honor, glory, and blessing! Hallelujah!!!

THE MOTIVATION, MESSAGE AND MEANING BEHIND THE MUSIC

Table of Contents

Introduction 17

Chapter I - Holy Is The Lamb 21

Chapter II - I Just Want To Praise You 35

Chapter III - Shout For Joy 51

Chapter IV - Greater Is He 65

Chapter V - In Your Presence 83

Chapter VI - Your Glory 99

Chapter VII - Ask Of Me 119

Chapter VIII - Beauty For Ashes 129

Chapter IX - Now Is The Time 141

Chapter X - Zion 153

About The Author 171

Endnotes 174

Introduction

Can one song change your entire life? Can one song cause you to fast and pray, laying before God day after day? Can one song cause you to hear the Spirit of God with great clarity and direction for your life? Can one song cause you to have such peace and confidence that you truly feel as though you do not need to depend on another person ever again in your life? Can one song open your spiritually blinded eyes and your spiritually deaf ears? Can one song cause you to return to your first love? Yes! That is what happened to me. Over seven years ago the Lord gave me a prophetic song that has changed my life. Because of that one song, this book exists. I never set out to write a book but when I recorded that one song, I began to see CDs, books, videos and so much more.

One day I asked, "Why did I not record the song earlier?" I heard my spirit say, "*And the Lord answered me, and said, Write the vision, and make it plain upon tables, that he may run that readeth it.*" *(Habakkuk 2:2)* I did not understand at first but after meditating on this scripture for several days, it came to me. In other words, something powerful happens when you take a thought and not only write it down but you meditate on that thought day and night until it becomes so real to you, that you are motivated to do whatever it takes to manifest that thought in the natural. I wrote down the thought seven years ago but I gave it to someone else to meditate on. I should have kept the recording for myself until I was ready to take it to the next level. Therefore, the song remained as a thought to me until now.

How many times have you thought of a new invention or idea and left it at just that - a thought. You never went to the next level to investigate or to research on what it takes to manifest that thought in the natural. Then one day you hear or see someone on the television or the radio that had the same thought, except they acted on that thought and now they are extremely prosperous?

I am acting on my thought now. Now is the time. I began this book December 6, 2003 and five weeks later it was completed. I heard the voice of God clearer than I ever have before. The Holy Spirit guided me the entire time and brought people, prophesies and scriptures back to my remembrance. Oh yes there were many distractions, but I had to stay focused. I would hear one word in my spirit and after seeking understanding, it turned into an entire chapter. It was difficult to shut down my computer and go to bed at night because out of my belly were flowing rivers of living water. I could not wait to get out of bed the next morning to write or read the scripture(s) that the Holy Spirit gave me during the night to include in this book. This is just the beginning. This book is the fundamentals of Christianity. I believe that God is going to allow me to move even more in the supernatural like never before.

I pray that you enjoy reading *"The Motivation, Message and Meaning Behind The Music."* I openly expose my heart on each page of this book as I intimately share how I received each song from the Holy Spirit, it's meaning and what I hear when I sing the songs from my self-titled project, *"Maranda Forney."* You will also see the hidden secret that God has revealed to me that will change your life!!!

As a result of recording the vision, I have been running since with so many dreams and visions. If you go on to read *Habakkuk 2:3* it states, *"For the vision is yet for an appointed time, but at the end it shall speak, and not lie: though it tarry, wait for it; because it will surely come, it will not tarry.* I believe that now is the appointed time to release all that God has invested in me. Once I recorded *"Holy Is the Lamb,"* the vision became clear and it began to speak to me and did not lie!

Chapter I – Holy Is The Lamb
The Motivation

As You sit at the right-hand

of your Father

there are angels surrounding You

We your people in the earth

lift-up our hands to You

Singing Holy, Holy is the Lamb

In 1996, during a Sunday morning service at All Nations Church in Columbus, Ohio, there was a personal and corporate experience of God like no other. I remember the praise and worship being extremely high that when you walked into the sanctuary, you immediately wanted to join in the singing and dancing. There was such energy and excitement in worshipping God, an atmosphere of expectancy was created. To be honest, I cannot tell you what was preached that day or even the songs that were ministered but I do remember a special moment in time that would change my life!

The congregation began to pray in the Spirit and that is when it happened! The corporate praying began to get louder and louder until we all sounded like one thunderous voice. Over 600 people praying in tongues to God the Father. I noticed that as I prayed, something took over my tongue and I could no longer fully control it. The unknown words that I was speaking began to get faster and faster and I could feel that something was about to happen. Suddenly I noticed a voice stood out in the congregation. Everyone began to lower their voices to hear the individual. After praying for a minute or two, the words, "An interpretation will come," were spoken.

There was a Holy silence in the sanctuary and then I heard,

"As You sit at the right-hand

of your Father

there are angels surrounding You

We your people in the earth

lift-up our hands to You

Singing Holy, Holy is the Lamb"

I immediately sat down and opened my bible to find a clean page to write the words down. I kept looking around to see if anyone else could hear what I was hearing. The words and the melody were so strong and so real to me.

After several minutes of silence, Pastor Williams asked the congregation, "Who has the

THE MOTIVATION, MESSAGE AND MEANING BEHIND THE MUSIC

interpretation?" I wanted to run to the front of the church and say, "Pastor, I have the interpretation," but I did not. After service, I went home and put the song on a cassette tape and gave it to Pastor during our evening service.

Over seven years have gone by and each day I think about that moment and/or the song. I still experience the same expectancy that I did then. My husband and my children sing the song all the time and my son Joseph who is only a year old, lifts his hands to worship when he hears the song. Out of all the songs that God has given me, this song is the strongest in my spirit. I often wake-up in the middle of the night to find my spirit singing, "Holy Is The Lamb."

I knew that I had to record this song. I felt that I needed to have a physical manifestation of the song. Once I went into the studio to record, I could begin to see the vision. I thank God that over the years, He has placed the right people around me to get it all done. One person in particular is my producer Greg Landfair.

I met Greg and his wonderful wife, Valerie in 1998 when my husband and I moved to Chicago, Illinois. He was the head musician for New Wine Church, pastored by Tom Bynum. I have met many musicians over the years but none like Greg. He is such a skilled musician and yet extremely humble. He is a true worshipper and he is able to make any guitar sing.

I recorded a scratch vocal of the song and gave to Greg. Within a week's time, Greg recorded the music and when I heard it for the first time, I was moved with emotion because it was so much more than what I expected.

Within a week Greg recorded the background vocals and a week later I recorded my vocals.

The Meaning

Over the last twelve years, I have had the opportunity to sit under great men and women of God; Bishop Brian Keith and Prophetess Donna Williams, Pastor Lafayette Scales, Prophet Tom and Prophetess Samantha Bynum and Pastors Gregory and Grace Dickow. All are very sound teachers that walk in the five-fold ministry. I may use some of the information from their messages in this book but I look forward to researching the scriptures for myself. That is what I am most excited about! I know that by the time this book is completed, I will have grown spiritually and closer to God. I know that I will see Him in a new way and I can feel confident that what I include in this book has been validated and can be verified in the Word of God.

When I meet someone for the first time, I will often ask, "What is the meaning of your name?" I think that it is very important to understand what you are speaking over someone. For instance, my name is Maranda Marie Forney. Maranda means, "Someone who is admired or adored; the beautiful one." However, Marie means, "rebellion." I do not tell people my middle name because I do not want them speaking over me the word "rebellion".

Just the same, when I am singing and ministering unto the Lord, I want to know what am

I saying. What am I truly singing when I tell God that He is the Alpha and the Omega, the Everlasting Father, the Prince of Peace, the King of Kings and the Lord of Lords? If I say, "Hallelujah!" I want to understand that I am saying "praise Jah," "praise ye Jehovah!" If I do not truly understand what I am saying, then how can I perceive who He is and worship God in spirit and in truth? *(John 4:24)* How can I perceive who I am?

When I sing unto God, "Holy is the Lamb," what am I saying to God? What are the seraphims saying in *Isaiah 6:3,* when they cried one to another, *"Holy, holy, holy, is the Lord of hosts: the whole earth is full of his glory,"* or in *Revelation 4:8,* when the four beasts that never rest are saying, *"Holy, holy, holy, Lord God Almighty, which was, and is, and is to come."*

I decided to research the scriptures to see if what I heard was truly of God. The more I learned, the more amazed and excited I became! I can truly say that I have heard from God!!!

While researching the word Holy, I found that Holy derived from the Old English word halig which is similar to the Old English word hal meaning whole or more at whole.[i] Holy is also a state of being set aside to the service of God. In the scriptures, the words rendered "Holy" (ha'gi̇os) denote separation to God.[ii]

According to the dictionary Holy is, "Exalted or worthy of complete devotion as one

THE MOTIVATION, MESSAGE AND MEANING BEHIND THE MUSIC

perfect in goodness and righteousness." So when I heard "Holy," I heard, Lord because of your righteousness, because you have been set aside and set apart, you are angelic, clean, consecrated, dedicated, devoted, divine, faithful, faultless, glorified, hallowed, immaculate, innocent, just, moral, perfect, pure, revered, sanctified, spotless, uncorrupt, undefiled, untainted, unworldly and upright! Praise God!

What about the word Lamb? I questioned should I record the song exactly as I heard it or should I change the word "Lamb" to "God". Initially, I was uncomfortable using the word Lamb due to a lack of understanding. It sounded like Jesus in His infancy, until I noticed several references of Lamb in the bible.

John the Baptist refers to Jesus twice as the Lamb of God in *John 1:29, "The next day John seeth Jesus coming unto him, and saith, Behold the Lamb of God, which taketh away the sin of the world."* And *John 1:36, "And looking upon Jesus as he walked, he saith, Behold the Lamb of God!"* I believe John referred to Jesus not as a young sheep that was weak or childlike but as someone who was sent as a sacrifice and whose death would have redeeming power.

What is "redeeming power?" To redeem means "to recover ownership of by paying a specified sum." It also means, "to set free; rescue or ransom." So John the Baptist realized that Jesus was no ordinary man, but the ransom or specified sum sent from God that was necessary to recover ownership of and rescue from satan an imprisoned people and restore them back to their original intended place of freedom, having all dominion and power.

In other words, in the beginning of creation, God created Adam in His image and after His likeness to have dominion over everything. (*Genesis 1:26*) God told Adam that he could eat of any tree in the Garden of Eden except for the tree of knowledge of good and evil. Adam and Eve disobeyed God and as a result were removed from the presence of God. The only person from that moment forward able to experience the Presence of God was the high priest after offering up to God, slaughtered goats and young bulls. Even then, it was only once a year on the Day of Atonement. So, in order for God to once again have a personal relationship with his people and restore them to their rightful place, he had to rescue them from sin and it's consequences by paying a ransom. The ransom had to be something or someone of great value. It had to be the greatest sacrifice there was. It had to be the Son of God, Jesus Christ. Therefore, Jesus Christ was born in the earth, suffered, died on the cross and rose from the dead to ascend into heaven to be seated with the Father.

In doing so, the people of God were restored back to where God had intended them to be from creation. All we have to do is believe in Jesus Christ and we have everlasting life! Jesus Christ, the Lamb of God who took away the sin of the world, is worthy to receive power, and riches, and wisdom, and strength, and honor, and glory, and blessing. (*Revelation 5:12*) Hallelujah!

Let us take a look at the word angel. Angel comes from the Greek word angelos, which means messenger.[iii] However, after studying the scriptures, I found that angels are more than messengers sent by God to deliver a word to man in the earth. They have different tasks and rank as well.

The archangel Michael is mentioned in *Revelation 12:7* where he and his angels were involved in warfare with satan, "*And there was war in heaven: Michael and his angels fought against the dragon; and the dragon fought and his angels.*" Michael having the title of archangel, means that he is a "chief" or "principle" angel. I also thought it was interesting that some angels had names and others did not. For example, the messenger sent from God to tell Mary that she would conceive Jesus, was named Gabriel. (*Luke 1:26*)

Two other types of angels that are mentioned throughout the bible are Cherubims and Seraphims. In *Genesis 3:24*, the Cherubims are guarding the tree of life with a flaming sword and in *Isaiah 6:2-3*, the Seraphims are standing above the throne crying, "*Holy, holy, holy.*"

What about the act of "lifting up your hands?" Throughout the scriptures you see the word hand or hands. In *Nehemiah 8:6,* Nehemiah blesses the Lord and the people lift up their hands. Hands are a symbol of who we are as well as our abilities. By lifting our hands toward heaven, we are saying, "God I surrender to Your power and Your dominion. All that I am and all that I am able to be and do, please take and have Your way O Lord! Let thy kingdom come and thy will be done in me."

THE MOTIVATION, MESSAGE AND MEANING BEHIND THE MUSIC

The Message

When I listen to *"Holy Is The Lamb,"* I can never just listen one time. I play the song over and over again. It is not that I love to hear myself sing, but that an atmosphere is being created each time the song plays. The atmosphere of the innercourt, the holy of holies, the most holy place where I commune with God on a deeper level of intimacy and He with me.

During the days of Ancient Israel, the Israelites called their sanctuary "the tabernacle of the congregation" *(Exodus 33:7)*. The tabernacle consisted of the altar of burnt offering, the brass laver, the court of the tabernacle *(Exodus 27:9)*, the holy place and the most holy or holy of holies. *(Exodus26:33)*

At the entrance of the tabernacle was the altar of burnt offering *(Exodus 27:1)* and just beyond the altar was a brass laver that the high priest would wash his hands and feet in before burning an offering. If the high priest did not wash as specified, he would die. *(Exodus 30:18-21)* He could then proceed to the holy place. Within the holy place was a table of shewbread *(Exodus 25:20-30)*, a seven-branched candlestick *(Exodus 25:31-39)*, and the altar of incense *(Exodus 30:1)*.

The altar of incense was to be placed right before the veil that hung between the holy place and the most holy. *(Exodus 30:1-6)* Within the most holy place was the Ark of the Covenant, the presence of God. (*Exodus 25:10-22*) Once a year, on the Day of Atonement, only the high priest could enter the most holy to offer a blood offering on behalf of himself and the sins of the people.

When Jesus Christ, the Lamb of God was sent as a ransom to redeem us from sin, He became the high priest. The earthly most holy then became a heavenly most holy and Jesus Christ the high priest would go to the Father on our behalf. That is why in *John 14:6* Jesus says, *"I am the way, the truth , and the life: no man cometh unto the Father, but by me."*

We now have everlasting life because of the Lamb of God! The blood of the Lamb has restored us back to our rightful place in the presence of God where we can commune with the Father anytime.

Once I understood the words that I received from the throne-room seven years ago, I then knew what God was saying.

Earlier I stated that in *Habakkuk 2:3*, it said, *"For the vision… shall speak, and not lie: though it tarry, wait for it; because it will surely come, it will not tarry."* Even though it took me seven years to understand, I now realize what the vision was saying. It is so simple but yet so profound.

Before Jesus gave himself as a sacrifice, the people of God had to rely on the high priest to go into the most holy once a year on their behalf for Atonement. When Jesus Christ died on the cross and became the ultimate high priest, the earthly most holy became a heavenly most holy and we were restored in His presence. The presence of God where God talks to us personally and we can talk to Him anytime we choose.

God wants us to realize that because He lives within us, we as believers already live in the holy of holies with Him. No matter how much or how well we sing, how graceful or how hard we dance, or how intense or how prolific we preach, that will not make us anymore righteous than we are now. It will not bring us into His presence. God provided that access when His blood was shed. However, we can experience deeper depths in Him as we sing psalms, hymns and spiritual songs, pray in the spirit and study and meditate on the Word of God. As we seek God and His righteousness, out of relationship with Him, we will experience greater power, and riches, and wisdom, and strength, and honor, and glory, and blessing. Hallelujah!

Chapter II – I Just Want To Praise You

The Motivation

I just want to praise You

Lift my hands and say, "I love You"

You mean everything to me

I exalt Your holy name

I exalt Your holy name

I exalt Your holy name on high

(by Arthur Tannous)

"*I Just Want To Praise You*" is the only song on this project that I did not write. Arthur Tannous wrote the song in 1987 and that is pretty much all that I know. I was unsuccessful in finding out more information about the writer and his motivation behind the song. So instead I will tell of my personal experience of the song and what message I receive when I minister this song unto the Lord.

It was sometime in the spring of 1997 when I first heard the song, "*I Just Want To Praise You.*" It was a Saturday morning when I entered the sanctuary of All Nations Church for Praise and Worship rehearsal, Bishop Williams instructed one of the keyboard players to teach me the song. It did not take long to learn at all. Even though I had never heard the song before, my spirit seemed to know the melody in some way. Though it is very simple, the message is powerful. In essence all I want to do is just praise God. I love to sing to Him! I love to dance before Him!! I love to clap my hands and shout unto the Lord!!!

I went home after rehearsal and I noticed that my spirit continued to minister, "*I Just Want To Praise You.*" During my "special time" with God, I began with, "*I Just Want To Praise You.*"

My husband and I moved to the Chicago, Illinois area, June 20, 1998 and every year we visit All Nations Church during their "Annual Family and Friends Picnic." Many times, Bishop Williams allows me to minister, and I sing, "*I Just Want To Praise You.*" One day while watching television, I saw Benny Hinn and he began to sing, "*I Just Want To Praise You.*"

In the Fall of 2000 my husband and I joined Life Changers International Church pastored by Pastors Gregory and Grace Dickow. During a Sunday morning service, the choir and praise team sang, "*I Just Want To Praise You.*"

November 30, 2001 my husband and I went to see Bishop Williams minister at Apostolic Faith

Church in Chicago, Illinois where Bishop Horace Brazier is the pastor. Bishop Williams called me up into the pulpit and I ministered, "*I Just Want To Praise You.*"

Because I have ministered the song so many times in the past, corporately and personally, it has become a part of me and I felt it was appropriate to include in this project. The song is so very simple and can be sung in any setting. Whenever I minister, I always want to be sensitive to the time that I am allowed. If the Man or Woman of God tells me that I have a minute to sing I want to be sensitive to that time. However, if they say, "let God use you," then I can flow with however long the song is in my spirit. For both situations, I have learned that this song is appropriate.

The Meaning

For years I have talked about praise and praising God but I wanted to truly understand the concept of praise. The word praise derived from the Old English word preisen. It means, "To extol in words or song; to magnify; to glorify on account of perfections or excellent works; to do honor to; to display the excellence of;"

In *Genesis 29:35,* Leah conceived her fourth son, *"and she said, Now will I praise the LORD: therefore she called his name Judah; and left bearing."* To give some background information, Leah was the daughter of a man named Laban. Laban had two daughters, Leah and Rachel. Rachel was the younger of the two. One day while Rachel was giving water to her father's sheep, she met a man named Jacob. It turns out that Jacob and Laban were related, so Laban invited Jacob to live with him and work on his land. Because Jacob was in love with Rachel, he told Laban that he would work for Laban for seven years and in exchange he wanted to marry his youngest daughter Rachel. After the seven years, Laban secretly gave his oldest daughter Leah to marry Jacob. When Jacob realized that it was Leah, he questioned Laban. Laban told Jacob that it was not customary to give the youngest daughter before the oldest in marriage. Laban then told Jacob that he could also have Rachel in one week, if he would work an additional seven years.

THE MOTIVATION, MESSAGE AND MEANING BEHIND THE MUSIC

Jacob being in love with Rachel, worked another seven years for Laban. In the meantime, because Jacob favored Rachel, God closed her womb so that she could not bare children and blessed her sister Leah. That is why in *Genesis 29:35*, Leah praised God and named her son Judah. Judah means praise. She thought by having four sons, and her sister Rachel having no children, this would cause her husband to love her as Rachel. Leah's response to God for what He had done was to praise Him.

That is what praise is, a response to God for what He has done. There are many ways to praise God. We can praise Him with our mouths as in *Psalms 34:1, "I will bless the Lord at all times: his praise shall continually be in my mouth."* We can praise Him with uplifted hands as in *Psalms 134:2, "Lift up your hands in the sanctuary, and bless the Lord."* We can praise God by clapping our hands as in *Psalms 47:1, "O clap your hands, all ye people;..."* And finally in *Psalms 150:3-5,* we praise God with *"the sound of the trumpet...the psaltery and harp...the timbrel... with stringed instruments and organs."*

Let's take a closer look at the ways to praise God. Many times we will praise God with the word, "Hallelujah" which means "praise Jehovah." *Hallel* comes from the Hebrew word *Halal* which means "to be boastful or to celebrate with great enthusiasm and joy." Halal praise is praising God like a madman. It is when you get to a place where you fully focus on God and all that He has done that you do not care who is watching or what people will say. It is when you are so full of praise for God that it overflows onto others like in *Psalms 34:23, "My soul shall make its boast in the Lord; the humble shall hear it and rejoice. O magnify the Lord with me, and let us exalt His name together."*

Yadah praise is praising God with extended hands. In *2 Chronicles 20:19-21*, Yadah praise is exhibited when the Levites of Kohath and Korah stood up to praise the Lord with a loud voice on high. Early the next morning the people went forth into the wilderness of Tekoa, and Jehoshaphat stood and said, *"Hear me, O Judah, and ye inhabitants of Jerusalem; Believe in the Lord your God, so shall ye be established; believe his prophets, so shall ye prosper."* In other words, if the children of Israel put their trust in the Lord God, stand their ground and believe what His prophets tell them, they will be successful. Then he appointed singers to sing praises unto the Lord while the army marched saying, *"Praise the Lord; for his mercy endureth forever."* Yadah praise is an act of our will where we choose to surrender to God for victory in God.

Towdah praise is praising God with thanksgiving. It carries an attitude of gratitude for the Lord. Towdah literally means, "an extension of the hand in adoration or acceptance." Towdah praise is used for thanking God for "things not yet received" as well as things already received. It is praising God now in faith before you receive your requests. It is a sacrificial praise as in *2 Chronicles 29:31*, where King Hezekiah commanded the Levites to, *"come near and bring sacrifices and*

THE MOTIVATION, MESSAGE AND MEANING BEHIND THE MUSIC

thank offerings into the house of the Lord," because God turned away His fierce wrath from them due to the sins of their fathers.

Shabach praise is praising God with a shout. It literally means "to shout, to address in a loud tone, to command, to triumph." In *Psalms 47:1*, it states, *"O clap your hands, all ye people; shout unto God with the voice of triumph."*

Barak praise is praising with expectation of receiving something from the Lord. Barak means "to kneel down, to bless God as an act of adoration." In *Judges 5:1-2*, the prophetess Deborah and Barak, the son of Abinoam sang, *"Praise ye the Lord for the avenging of Israel, when the people willingly offered themselves."*

Zamar praise is praising God with musical instruments. Zamar means "to touch the strings" refers to worshipping with musical instruments. In *Psalms 98:4-6* it says to, *"Make a joyful noise unto the Lord, all the earth; make a loud noise, and rejoice, and sing praise. Sing unto the Lord with the harp; with the harp, and the voice of a Psalms. With trumpets and sound of cornet make a joyful noise before the Lord, the King."*

Tehillah praise is praising God spontaneously. Tehillah is derived from the word Halal and means "the singing of halals, to sing or to laud; perceived to involve music, especially singing; hymns of the Spirit." A hymn is a song of praise or thanksgiving to God. A hymn of the Spirit is a song of praise or thanksgiving to God given of the Holy Spirit. In essence it is a spiritual song. A song that is unrehearsed and unprepared. This was demonstrated in Exodus the 15th chapter when Moses and Miriam both praised God spontaneously when God delivered the children of Israel from Pharaoh.

In the New Testament, there are five different Greek words for praise; Psallo, Hymneo, Epaineo, Eulogeo and Aineo. Psallo according to Strong's # 5567, means "to twitch or twang; i.e. to play on a stringed instrument (celebrate the divine worship with music and accompanying odes)."

Hymneo according to Strong's # 5214 is a verb from the noun humnos, and Strong says it literally means "to hymn, i.e. sing a religious ode; by implication, to celebrate (God) in song."

Epaineo according to Strong's # 1868 is a strengthened form of Aineo and denotes approbation, commendation, and praise. It is used of those on account of, and by reason of, whom as God's heritage, praise is to be ascribed to God, in respect of His glory.

Eulogetos according to Strong's # 2128 means blessed, praised; it is only applied to God. The root of Eulogetos is Eulogeo. "Eu" means "to be well off, to prosper, to praise, or speak good of." "Logos" means "word: the Word of God."

Aineo according to Strong's # 136 means "to extol; to sing praises in honor to God, or to offer thanksgiving." This praise done enthusiastically to catch the attention of God.

THE MOTIVATION, MESSAGE AND MEANING BEHIND THE MUSIC

The Message

I am not sure what Arthur Tannous' motivation was behind writing, "*I Just Want To Praise You,*" but the meaning and message behind the song are very powerful. Praise is a response to God for what He has done. Because God has done so many wonderful things for me, it is natural that I want to praise Him. Not only has He done great things but He continues to do so much that it literally "blows my mind!" When I think on these things, as the song says, I lift my hands and say, "I love you" because He is everything to me.

When I think of the word everything, I think of His many names.
- El Shaddai meaning God Almighty or God All Sufficient. Having absolute power; all-powerful.
- Adonai meaning Lord.
- Jehovah Adon Kal Ha'arets meaning The Lord of All the Earth.
- Jehovah Bara meaning The Lord Creator.
- Jehovah Chatsahi meaning The Lord My Strength.
- Jehovah Chereb meaning The Lord…the Sword.
- Jehovah Eli meaning The Lord My God.
- Jehovah Elyon meaning The Lord Most High.
- Jehovah 'Ez-Lami meaning The Lord My Strength.
- Jehovah Gador Milchamah meaning The Lord Mighty in Battle.
- Jehovah Ganan meaning The Lord Our Defense.

- Jehovah Go'el meaning The Lord Thy Redeemer.
- Jehovah Hashopet meaning The Lord the Judge.
- Jehovah Hoshe'ah meaning The Lord Save.
- Jehovah "Immeku meaning The Lord Is with you.
- Jehovah 'Izoz Hakaboth meaning The Lord Strong and Mighty.
- Jehovah Jireh meaning The Lord Will Provide.
- Jehovah Kabodhi meaning The Lord My Glory.
- Jehovah Kanna meaning The Lord Whose Name is Jealous.
- Jehovah Keren-Yish'I meaning The Lord The Horn of My Salvation.
- Jehovah Machsi meaning The Lord My Refuge.
- Jehovah Magen meaning The Lord, the Shield.
- Jehovah Ma'oz meaning The Lord…My Fortress.
- Hamelech Jehovah meaning The Lord the King.
- Jehovah Melech 'Olam meaning The Lord King Forever.
- Jehovah Mephalti meaning The Lord My Deliverer.
- Jehovah M'gaddishcem meaning The Lord Our Sanctifier.
- Jehovah Metsodhathi meaning The Lord…My Fortress.
- Jehovah Misqabbi meaning The Lord My High Tower.
- Jehovah Naheh meaning The Lord that Smiteth.
- Jehovah Nissi meaning The Lord Our Banner.
- Jehovah 'Ori meaning The Lord My Light.

THE MOTIVATION, MESSAGE AND MEANING BEHIND THE MUSIC

- Jehovah Rapha meaning The Lord that Healeth.
- Jehovah Rohi meaning The Lord My Shepherd.
- Jehovah Sabaoth meaning The Lord of Hosts.
- Jehovah Sel'i meaning The Lord My Rock.
- Jehovah Shalom meaning The Lord Our Peace.
- Jehovah Shammah meaning The Lord Is There.
- Jehovah Tiskenu meaning The Lord Our Righteousness.
- Jehovah Tsori meaning O Lord My Strength.
- Jehovah Yasha meaning The Lord, thy Saviour.

Another name for everything, which actually embodies all of the names, is Jesus. When we call on the name of Jesus, we are calling all of the names of Jehovah, El Shaddai and Adonai.

At one time or another, God has been all of this to me and more. He has been my Jehovah Jireh and provides for me at all times. There have even been instances when my back was up against the wall and I literally did not know where my next meal would come from. I remember one particular instance, in 1992, my husband and I were low on money and had to make the choice of paying our tithes or buying dinner for ourselves and two small children. We paid our tithes and rejoiced in the Lord throughout the service. Then at the end of service, Pastor Williams asked my husband if we wanted to join he and his family for dinner. That evening we ended up going to a very nice restaurant and Pastor paid for our entire meal. God was faithful that day in being our Jehovah Jireh and supplying our dinner. We never said anything to

Pastor about our situation but God placed it on his heart to buy our dinner.

There have been many times that God has been my Jehovah Tsori, my God of strength. When I decided to go back to school in 1991, I majored in engineering. Being a male dominated field, often I would be the only female in my class. This one particular class I had a professor that believed a women's place was in the kitchen, bare-foot and pregnant. In fact, he told me so. My professor did everything that he could to discourage me and there were many nights that I would sit in my car and cry. I wanted to quit and give up but I kept hearing, *Philippians 4:13, "I can do all things through Christ which strengtheneth me."* God was and is faithful and strengthened me not to just complete that class, but I finished with an "A."

God has also been my Jehovah Rapha. In 1999, my oldest son Michael Elisha suddenly began to experience seizures. The first time that he had one, he was at the daycare and just as my husband and I were picking him up, we saw the ambulance. When I noticed that it was my son on the stretcher, initially I panicked. We followed the ambulance to the hospital and after several tests, they could not tell us why he would suddenly begin to have seizures at the age of six. We experienced two other episodes after the initial seizure before seeking a specialist. They prescribed a medication called dilantin, which had several side effects. One of them causing your gums to become very sore. Everytime Michael would cry because of his gums,

THE MOTIVATION, MESSAGE AND MEANING BEHIND THE MUSIC

my heart cried out to God. Then one day the Lord led me to *Matthew 17:14-21*. It talked about a man who had a son that would act like a lunatic and would oftentimes fall in the fire and water. As I read, it reminded me of when Michael would have seizures. His little body would begin to convulse very violently for a minute or two and then he would fall asleep remembering nothing that had happened. When I went on to read, the man told Jesus that the disciples were not able to heal his son. Jesus then rebuked the devil, the devil left the child and the child was healed. When the disciples asked why they could not cast out the devil, Jesus said, *"because of your unbelief: for verily I say unto you, If ye have faith as a grain of mustard seed, ye shall say unto this mountain, Remove hence to yonder place; and it shall remove; and nothing shall be impossible unto you. Howbeit this kind goeth not out but by prayer and fasting."* When I read that scripture, the number one thing that stuck out in my mind was, "by prayer and fasting." I shared this with my husband and we both set ourselves in agreement. We fasted and prayed and then we decided to lay hands on our son. The next step was to act in faith and we took my son off of the medication and praised God for the healing. Thank God I can say that from that day on, we never gave Michael any more medication and he never had another seizure. It has been over four years! Hallelujah!

    I can go on and on about how God has personally been one of the many names listed. When I sing *"I Just Want To Praise You"* these are the things that I think about. I think of His goodness and His lovingkindness, His grace and His mercies, which are new every morning!!!

Finally, I love to sing "*I Just Want To Praise You*," because it touches so many levels of praise. I can sing this song when I am offering up Yadah praise with my hands extended, Towdah praise because I sing with a heart of thanksgiving and Barak praise when I kneel down and bless God in adoration.

It also represents Epaineo praise because it denotes warm approval, Eulogetos praise which speaks good of the Word of God which is God and Aineo praise, which means to extol and sing, praises in honor to God.

THE MOTIVATION, MESSAGE AND MEANING BEHIND THE MUSIC

Chapter III – Shout For Joy

The Motivation

I will praise You O Lord

With my whole heart

I will tell of Your wonders

Be glad and rejoice

Shout, shout for joy

And be glad

For Your favor and righteousness

Have caused me to magnify you O Lord

"Shout For Joy" is actually a combination of two spiritual songs. I received the verse in September of 1999 and the chorus in September of 2001.
September of 1999 my husband and I were members of New Wine Church pastored by Pastor Tom and Prophetess Samantha Bynum. At the time we were having our Sunday morning services at a

mall located in the far south side of Chicago. I had only been leading worship for a couple of months. I remember my spirit being very uplifted and vibrant that morning. The intercessors began praying while the team stood to the side waiting for one additional member to arrive. I joined in with the intercessors and prayed while Greg and the band played lightly behind the intercessors. Words came to my spirit to the beat of the music and after a minute or so; I sang the words very softly to myself. When I opened my eyes to see if our worship leader had arrived, to my surprise, she had not and our associate pastor looked at me to lead worship. The team was already standing in place at the microphone and I raced to take the lead mic. Greg continued to play and I began to sing:

I will praise You O Lord

With my whole heart

I will tell of Your wonders

Be glad and rejoice

    I was so excited because we were singing a spiritual song and giving Tehillah praise. We were praising God spontaneously. Soon the team joined in and 10 minutes within singing the song, I heard our worship leader adding harmony. We had no set pattern, just whenever I had an unction in my spirit to repeat a phrase or word, the team followed.

    The congregation joined in and there was such freedom in the atmosphere. I felt so free that I began to dance back and forth across the floor, spinning and lifting my hands. At times, Greg changed the sound and momentum of the music and we literally traveled around the world with that one song. We started out gradually, building momentum until it was pulsating and vigorous. Every now and then we would rest allowing only the musicians to play and then we would take off again to a new destination. We went from the United States, down to Central America and experienced a little of Costa Rica on down to the fertile lowland of Columbia where is was hot and rainy. We continued to travel southeast to Brazil atop Corcovado Mountain where the statue of Christ is, on out through the southernmost town on the planet, Ushuaia on Tierra del Fuego in Argentina. We swam with the whales and played with the penguins and seals in Antarctica and turned up toward Australia (the land down under) where we stopped at the Sydney Opera House in Sydney Harbor. After jumping from Indonesia, to Singapore, to Malaysia, to the Philippines, we rested in Vietnam for a moment and then we were off again through Cambodia and Thailand where we crossed the Indian Ocean to praise with our brothers and sisters in India. We headed north and jumped over the Great Wall of China into Mongolia. From there, east to the Kolyma Mountains and then crossed the Arctic Ocean and landed in Norway on down through Sweden and Finland to rest in Moscow. We visited the Kremlin and then we were off again to France where we sang "Bon Jour" to our French brothers and sisters and "Hola" to our

Spanish brothers and sisters in Spain. Finally we traveled through the Sahara Desert to Egypt down through Sudan, Kenya, Tanzania and Zimbabwe to stop and eat in South Africa before crossing the Atlantic Ocean to head back to Chicago, Illinois.

Almost two years later to the date, while at Life Changers International Church where Pastors Gregory and Grace Dickow are the pastors, my husband and I were sitting in the back of the church taking notes as Pastor Dickow taught on "Financial Freedom." He told the congregation to turn to *Psalms 35:27* and read, *"Let them shout for joy, and be glad, that favour my righteous cause: yea, let them say continually, Let the Lord be magnified, which hath pleasure in the prosperity of his servant."* My spirit lit-up and I began to hear:

Shout, shout for joy

And be glad

For Your favor and righteousness

Have caused me to magnify you O Lord

My thoughts were so consumed with this chorus that I did not hear the rest of the message. I could not wait until service concluded so that I could sing the chorus out loud and hear clearly what my spirit was singing. After service while in the car, I said to my children and husband, "Listen everyone, the Lord gave me another song." I began to sing the chorus and after the fourth or fifth time, I noticed that I naturally flowed right into the verse that I had received two years previously at New Wine Church. My family joined in and we sang the entire song the whole way home.

The Meaning

The verse, "I will praise You, O Lord, with my whole heart; I will tell of Your wonders, be glad and rejoice" can be found in *Psalms 9:1-2*. This is a Messianic Psalms of David. Messianic meaning "of or relating to a messiah." And this Psalms is unto the chief Musician upon Muth-labben. Muth-labben means "the death of the son" or "on the death of the man who came forth from between the camps," alluding to Goliath, the Philistine.

To elaborate, in *1 Samuel chapter 17*, there was a battle going on between Israel and Philistia in the Valley of Elah. The Israelites were afraid to fight the Philistines because they had one soldier that was over nine feet tall and his name was Goliath. To give an idea of Goliath's strength, the bible says that his helmet was made of bronze and he wore a breastplate that weighed 5000 shekels of bronze. A shekel is the common standard both of weight and value among the Hebrews. It is estimated at 220 English grains, or a little more than half an ounce. So if the breastplate weighed 5000 shekels and a shekel is equal to a little more than half an ounce, then the breastplate weighed 2500 ounces or over 156 pounds. It also goes on to say that his legs and shoulders were covered with bronze and the spearhead of his spear weighed 600 shekels or over 18 pounds. Goliath challenged the Israelites and would say, *"Why are ye come out to set your battle in array? am not I a Philistine, and ye servants to Saul? choose you a man for you, and let him come down to me. If he be able to fight with me, and to kill me, then will we be your servants: but if I prevail against him, and kill him, then shall ye be our servants, and serve us."* (1 Samuel 17:8-9) He then went on to say, *"I defy the armies of Israel this day; give me a man, that we may fight together."* (1 Samuel 17:10)

The bible says that when Saul and his army heard what Goliath had said, they were greatly afraid and discouraged. It was not until a young shepherd boy named David came along. David's father Jesse, told David to take some food to his three older brothers who were part of the Israelites fighting the Philistines. David arrived and just as his brothers were going out to fight, Goliath came up and challenged the Israelites again. The bible says in *1 Samuel 17:24, "And all the men of Israel, when they saw the man, fled from him, and were sore afraid."* David questioned the men in disbelief that they would be afraid of a man who defied the armies of the living God. When King Saul heard of what David was saying, he sent for him. David told Saul that he would fight the Philistine. Saul tried to discourage David because he was only a young boy and Goliath was a giant man but David did not listen. David told Saul, *"The Lord that delivered me out of the paw of the lion, and out of the paw of the bear, he will deliver me out of the hand of this Philistine."* (1 Samuel 17:37) In other words, if God delivered David from being killed by a lion and bear when his sheep were being attacked, then why wouldn't he deliver him from a mere man that has threatened and challenged the people of God or in essence, God Himself.

Saul blesses David and gives him his armor. David could not walk and took it off. With only his staff, five smooth stones and his sling, he confronted Goliath.

When Goliath saw David he said, *"Am I a dog, that you come to me with sticks?"* Then Goliath cursed David by his gods and said, *"Come to me, and I will give your flesh to the birds of the air and the beasts of the field!"* (*1 Samuel 17:43-44,* NKJ*)*

But in *1 Samuel 17:45-47* NKJ, David says to Goliath, *"You come to me with a sword, with a spear, and with a javelin. But I come to you in the name of the Lord of hosts, the God of the armies of Israel, whom you have defied. This day the Lord will deliver you into my hand, and I will strike you and take your head from you. And this day I will give the carcasses of the camp of the Philistines to the birds of the air and the wild beasts of the earth, that all the earth may know that there is a God in Israel. Then all this assembly shall know that the Lord does not save with sword and spear; for the battle is the Lord's and He will give you into our hands."*

Goliath headed toward David and David hurried toward Goliath. David took one of his stones and slung it and struck Goliath in the forehead. Goliath fell and David took Goliath's sword and cut off his head. In *1 Samuel 17:51-52* NKJ it says, *"...And when the Philistines saw that*

THE MOTIVATION, MESSAGE AND MEANING BEHIND THE MUSIC

their champion was dead, they fled. Now the men of Israel and Judah arose and shouted, and pursued the Philistines as far as the entrance of the valley..."

The Message

When I sing *"Shout For Joy,"* I hear the words Halal, Yadah, Shabach and Towdah. Halal meaning "to be boastful or to celebrate with great enthusiasm and joy." In *Psalms 34:2* it says, *"My soul shall make her boast in the Lord..."* My soul will be proud in the Lord. Because of the great things He has done, I can praise God with confidence and pride.

I hear Yadah meaning "with extended hands." As I extend my hands to praise God with a loud voice on high, believe in the Lord my God, believe his prophets, then I will have victory in God. (*2 Chronicles 20:20*)

Shabach meaning "with a shout. I am shouting to God for causing me to triumph." In *2 Corinthians 2:14* it says, *"Now thanks be unto God, which always causeth us to triumph in Christ."*

Towdah meaning "with thanksgiving." I am thanking God for "things not yet received" as well as things already received. I am praising God now in faith before I receive my request. In *Philippians 4:6* we are to be careful for nothing; but in every thing by prayer and supplication with thanksgiving let our requests be made known unto God."

We all have a Goliath in our lives that appears to be bigger than we can perceptually handle. This Goliath that we pray to God to deliver us from, is a strong man and if we would be like David, see the Goliath for who he is, an uncircumcised Philistine, then we will experience the victory that God has already promised! The Goliaths in our lives are many times intimidating and embarrassing to face. But if we would allow the Holy Spirit to show us those hidden places and we seek understanding, then we can overcome them. For me, my Goliath was in the area of my finances. No matter how much money I made, I continued to stay in debt, until now. The bible clearly says in *Romans 13:8* to owe no man anything but love. When Pastor Dickow taught on Financial Freedom and what steps we needed to take to not only be debt free but to be prosperous, my spirit-man rejoiced giving Towdah praise unto the Lord. Through Pastor Dickow, the Holy Spirit revealed to me how to conquer financial frustration. Pastor Dickow taught from *Haggai 1:5-6*, *"Now therefore thus saith the Lord of hosts; Consider your ways. You have sown much and bring in little; you eat, but do not have enough; you drink, but you are not filled with drink; you clothe yourselves, but no one is warm; and he who earns wages, earns wages to put into a bag with holes."* In other words, we sow much but reap little, we eat, but never seem to have enough, we have clothes and shelter, but it seems like a struggle and we earn wages but the money seems to disappear so quickly.

Pastor Dickow said that this was poverty and lack, which is not having enough. He then referred to *John 10:10* where it says, *"The thief cometh not, but for to steal, and to kill, and to destroy: I am come that they might have life, and that they might have it more abundantly."* God desires for us to live a life full of abundance in all areas. Many times we have an abundance in one area and experience lack in another. Many times people experience lack because they get desperate and put themselves in a tight position. A response to being in this state is to take shortcuts and not do things God's way. But *Matthew 6:33* says, *"But seek first the kingdom of God (His way of doing things) and His righteousness and all these things shall be added to you."*

Chapter IV – Greater Is He

The Motivation

People let me tell you something

satan only comes to steal, kill, destroy

You've got to be stronger

When you're going through trials to seek the Lord

The devil is deceiving

He'll approach you in ways you'd never think

But one thing you have to remember

He is just the enemy

Greater is He that lives within me than he that is in the world

We are fighting a spiritual war so keep your mind on the Lord

Greater is He that lives within me than he that is in the world

We are fighting a spiritual war so keep your eyes on the Lord

satan get thee behind me

Take your hands off my sister release my brother

I shall fear no evil

As I walk through the valley of death I will trust my Father

For God so loved the world that He gave

His only Son to die for me

That who believes in Him

Shall not parish but live eternally

We wrestle not against flesh and blood

But against principalities

Rulers of darkness and spiritual wickedness

For my God is more powerful than all of them

    It was 1992, a babe in Christ and on fire for God, I shared my rebirth with everyone who would listen. I became active in my church by joining the choir and praise team and I loved reading the Word of God. By this time I had written two songs, *"Seekingly Yours"* about a teenage girl who wanted to have an abortion and *"Tell Me"* a rap about the youth of today. It seemed like the more I read the bible, the more songs I heard. I remember being ecstatic and thinking, "I could have over a million songs if I keep studying the Word."

At the time I worked for an insurance company headquartered in Columbus, Ohio. The atmosphere was very stringent and management wanted us to live, breathe, and sleep, productivity. You could not use the telephone unless it was an absolute emergency and you were told when you could go on break and take lunch. Even though I had accepted Jesus Christ as my personal Lord and Savior, my mind needed to be renewed. I was very feisty at that time and my manager and I were constantly arguing. She did not believe in being discreet and enjoyed reprimanding her employees in front of others. I lived in the personnel department filing complaint after complaint which got me no where fast.

It was because of these circumstances that I decided to go back to school. I felt that having a college degree would allow me to have a career where I would not have to endure such harsh treatment. Little did I know. I learned over time that even with a college degree, you can still be spiritually imprisoned.

My job entailed reading letters from senior citizens who were not satisfied with the amount of money they received as a result of a medical claim being filed. I would review their claim to make sure the guidelines were properly followed. One day while sitting at my desk reviewing a claim, my spirit sang:

Greater is He that lives within me than He that is in the world

We are fighting a spiritual war so keep your eyes on the Lord

Greater is He that lives within me than He that is in the world

We are fighting a spiritual war so keep your mind on the Lord

I was so excited and I could not wait to get off from work so that I could sing the song aloud and hear what my spirit was singing. When the clock struck 3:30, I raced to shut down my computer and out the door I ran. My husband worked just two floors above me and we met in the lobby and walked to our car together. When I saw him I said, "I have a new song, do you want to hear it?" Of course he had no choice. When I sang the chorus, he responded, "That's tight." I kept singing the chorus in hope that more would come. We stopped to pick our children up from the baby-sitter and when we arrived home, out of my belly flowed rivers of living water. When I wrote down the chorus, then the verses came:

People let me tell you something

satan only comes to steal, kill, destroy

THE MOTIVATION, MESSAGE AND MEANING BEHIND THE MUSIC

You've got to be stronger

When you're going through trials to seek the Lord

The devil is deceiving

He'll approach you in ways you'd never think

But one thing you have to remember

He is just the enemy

I kept singing this verse and chorus over and over again until I had it memorized. Then I heard the second verse:

satan get thee behind me

Take your hands off my sister release my brother

I shall fear no evil

As I walk through the valley of death I will trust my Father

For God so loved the world that He gave

His only Son to die for me

That who believes in Him

Shall not parish but live eternally

The following Saturday before choir practice, I taught the song to my friends and sisters-in-the-Lord; Angela Bosman, Darla Kelso and

Wanda Chambers. Angela is the harmony queen. She can add harmony to any song and she has an excellent ear for pitch. In fact Angela is probably the only person in Columbus who knows all the songs that God has given to me. She was always the first person of all my friends that I would go to when God gave me a new song. We would spend hours just singing and harmonizing.

I did not add the bridge until recently after reading *Ephesians 6:12*:

We wrestle not against flesh and blood

But against principalities

Rulers of darkness and spiritual wickedness

For my God is more powerful than all of them

The Meaning

"*Greater Is He*," completely lines up with the Word of God, in fact it is the Word of God entirely. Beginning with the 1st verse:

People let me tell you something

satan only comes to steal, kill, destroy

This comes from *John 10:10, "The thief cometh not, but for to steal, and to kill, and to destroy..."* A thief is someone who steals. satan is a thief because he comes to steal our body, kill our soul and destroy our spirit. He does not want us to understand that we were created in God's image and after His likeness and that we have dominion over every living thing.

You've got to be stronger

When you're going through trials to seek the Lord

That is why we are to, "*seek ye first the kingdom of God, and his righteousness;...*" (*Matthew 6:33*) to understand the will of God for our lives. We will see that our steps are already planned out for us and ordered of the Lord. (*Psalms 37:23*) If we do not know and understand the plan of God for our lives, many times we invite confusion from making choices that do not line-up with God's plan. At that point, we are no longer walking in the Spirit but in the "flesh". We can make it even worse by trying to "fix" the problem ourselves, in the flesh. But if we are strong in the Lord and in the power of His might (*Ephesians 6:10*) and we turn to Him and trust Him, then we will realize we already have the victory. The very thing that we fear, has already been conquered.

The devil is deceiving

He'll approach you in ways you'd never think

In *2 John 1:7* satan is called a deceiver and an antichrist. A deceiver is someone who leads you to believe something that is not true. He is a liar and the truth is not in him. In fact satan is the father of lies and he only gains access through our minds and in our thoughts, if we allow him.

But one thing you have to remember

He is just the enemy

Greater is He that lives within me than He that is in the world

We are fighting a spiritual war so keep your eyes on the Lord

Greater is He that lives within me than He that is in the world

We are fighting a spiritual war so keep your mind on the Lord

When Jesus Christ died on the cross, rose from the dead and ascended into heaven where he is seated with the Father, He overcame sin and defeated satan. Jesus is the great conquer! He is the only wise God and unto Him be glory and majesty, dominion and power, both now and forever. (*Jude 1:25*) He is the great I am, He is El-Shaddai, the Almighty God, He is more than enough, He is Omniscient, knowing all things and Omnipotent, having all power. Because He is all these things and more, Jesus is the Greatest and there is none greater. According to Webster's Revised Unabridged Dictionary, great means "to be endowed with extraordinary powers; uncommonly gifted; able to accomplish vast results; strong; powerful; mighty; and noble." I am so glad that I know Him and I serve the Greatest God.

In 2 *Timothy 1:7* it says, *"For God has not given us a spirit of fear, but of love, power, and a sound mind."* God has given us a sound mind to make sound and stable decisions. If our mind is overwhelmed and distracted from the things of God, then our defenses are down and our heart can be easily pierced. It is in the heart where Love lives and satan hates Love. He is jealous of Love and wants Love destroyed. So he plants a very subtle lie in our mind and even when we initially discard it, he will continue with that same lie as well as other lies until we are so bombarded with so many negative thoughts that we begin to accept the lie as being the truth. satan instigates and causes us to begin to see things that are not true. Our mind begins to create vivid pictures of an alleged situation of something that is not true. Before we know it, there is a battle going on in our minds but we get so caught up in the moment that we do not realize that it is all just a lie. That is why we have to cast down, throw down, destroy and deject every imagination, and every high thing that exalts itself against the knowledge of God, and bring into captivity every thought to the obedience of Christ. (*2 Corinthians 10:5*)

satan get thee behind me

Take your hands off my sister release my brother

In *Luke 4:1-8*, the Holy Spirit led Jesus into the wilderness where satan tempted Him for 40 days. Jesus had eaten nothing and satan came to Him and said, "*If You are the Son of God, command this stone to become bread.*" And Jesus replied, "*It is written, 'Man shall not live by bread alone, but by every word of God.*" And the devil took Jesus up to a high mountain and showed him all the kingdoms of the world in a moment of time and said, "*All this power will I give thee, and the glory of them: for that is delivered unto me; and to whomsoever I will I give it. If thou therefore wilt worship me, all shall be thine.*" Jesus answered and said, "*Get behind Me, satan! For it is written, 'You shall worship the Lord your God, and Him only you shall serve.'*"

I shall fear no evil

As I walk through the valley of death I will trust my Father

THE MOTIVATION, MESSAGE AND MEANING BEHIND THE MUSIC

Psalms 23:4 says, *"Yea, though I walk through the valley of the shadow of death, I will fear no evil..."* In other words, when I am facing a time of darkness or a time of uncertainty, I will not be afraid because God my shepherd will walk with me and at times carry me through the valley, which are the low times in my life. We are to be strong and of a good courage, fear not, nor be afraid, for the Lord our God is with us and he will not fail us, nor forsake us. (*Deuteronomy 31:6*)

For God so loved the world that He gave

His only Son to die for me

That who believes in Him

Shall not parish but live eternally

God loves us so much that he gave His only begotten Son, who was wounded for our transgressions and bruised for our iniquities, to redeem us from sin and now we have eternal life. (*John 3:16*) (*Isaiah 53:5*)

We wrestle not against flesh and blood

But against principalities

Rulers of darkness and spiritual wickedness

For my God is more powerful than all of them

Because the war that we are fighting is a spiritual war or a war of the mind, many times we will try to fight this war in the natural. We battle against powerful evil forces of fallen angels headed by satan who is a vicious fighter. But if we depend on God's strength and use every piece of his armor we will be victorious. The Holy Spirit will guide us and the armor of God will protect us. The armor of God is:

- Belt of Truth
- Breastplate of righteousness
- Shield of Faith
- Helmet of Salvation
- Sword of the Spirit
- Readiness to spread the gospel of peace

The Message

When I sing, *"Greater Is He,"* I hear warfare. Warfare is "the waging of war against an enemy; armed conflict." A war has been waged against satan and his demons in the heavenlies. This is a spiritual war and is fought in the mind of God's people. satan's weapon is lies and he can only gain access through our mind. satan is the father of lies and a deceiver. he bombards our minds with so many lies until it creates a picture that appears to be the truth but in reality, it too is only a lie. The good news is, we have already won the war. When Jesus Christ shed His blood and redeemed us from sin, we were restored back to our rightful place. Having dominion and power over every living thing. Having dominion and power over our minds. However many of us either do not know or do not realize that we already have this power and we allow satan to enter into our minds and tell us more lies. We cannot listen to the lies and forget what God has already spoken, but we must remember and understand that we are not fighting a man, but we are fighting evil spirits in high places and therefore we have to use spiritual weapons. Our spiritual weapon is the whole armor of God. When we put on the whole armor of God then we are able to cast down lies and false images that satan plants in our mind.

What is the whole armor of God? The armor of God is the belt of truth, the breastplate of righteousness, feet shod with the preparation of the gospel of peace, the shield of faith, the helmet of salvation, and the sword of the Spirit.

The belt of truth is the Word of God. The Word is the only truth, and we need to stand on the Word when adversity comes. We need to eat, sleep and breathe the Word of God, so when people see us, they do not see what we are wearing but they see the Word. Just as a belt is used to hold up clothing on our bodies, the Word of God is used to hold us up during our fiery trials. So during times of uncertainty, we can "tighten" our belt while standing on truths written in the Word of God. That is why it is important to meditate day and night on the Word of God, (*Psalms 1:2*) when we are tested, we will know the Word and can stand. The bible says in *2 Timothy 2:15*, *"Study to shew thyself approved unto God... rightly dividing the word of truth."*

The breastplate of righteousness is the confidence of being in right standing with God. When Jesus Christ shed His blood for our sins, we were made righteous or restored back to a right standing with God. All we had to do was confess with our mouths the Lord Jesus, and believe in our heart that God was raised from the dead, and we were saved. (*Romans 10:9*) By faith we are justified and in essence when God looks upon us, He no longer sees sin but the blood of Jesus Christ.

Feet shod with the preparation of the gospel of peace is being ready at all times to preach the Word of God and being ready in season and out of season. (*2 Timothy 4:2*) In fact God tells us to, "*Go ye into all the world, and preach the gospel to every creature.*" (*Mark 16:15*)

The shield of faith is living a life without fear. God has not given us a spirit of fear and does not want us to walk in fear because of what we see. God wants us to walk by faith. (*2 Corinthians 5:7*) Faith is the substance of things hoped for, the evidence of things not seen. (*Hebrews 11:1*) In other words, we are to keep hope alive when we do not see the promises that God made to us being fulfilled immediately, but know that God is not a man that He should lie and He will do what He said He would do. (*Numbers 23:19*) How do we get faith? We get it by hearing the Word of God. (*Romans 10:17*) Faith works love (*Galatians 5:6*) and there is no fear in Love, in fact perfect Love casts out fear. (*1 John 4:18*)

The helmet of salvation is the belief of salvation. *1 Thessalonians 5:8* says, "*...and for an helmet, the hope of salvation.*" Hope is a belief and salvation is saving power so in essence the helmet of salvation is a belief of saving power. The belief that God loved the world and gave His only begotten Son, that whosoever believes in Him shall not parish but have eternal life." (*John 3:16*)

The sword of the spirit is the spoken Word of God. Logos which is the Word of God (*Stong's #3056*) is used to identify the written scriptures in the bible, given under the inspiration of God. (*Timothy 3:16, 1 Peter 1:10-11*). Rhema which is the spoken Word of God (*Strong's #4487*) is or has been uttered by the living voice. It carries a spiritual connotation that differs from Logos. During our quiet time we read a verse that "speaks" directly to the situation we are dealing with, that portion of the scripture is a "*Rhema* word" from God for our situation. We can then stand in faith on the *Rhema* word, God has given us and confess it whenever satan tries to convince us otherwise.

THE MOTIVATION, MESSAGE AND MEANING BEHIND THE MUSIC

Chapter V – In Your Presence

The Motivation

In Your Presence

In Your Presence

In Your Presence is where I love to be

It's where I hear Your Voice

See Your Face

You tell me Your most intimate Thoughts

Your Presence is where I love to be

It's where You hold me close

Safe in Your Arms

Just You and I such intimacy

Your Presence is where I love to be

In Your Presence there is fullness of joy

At Your right-hand there are pleasures forever more

It was a cold Sunday morning, March 26, 2000 in Chicago, Illinois. During this time my husband and I were members of New Wine International Church where Pastors Tom and Prophetess Samantha Bynum were the pastors. As a result of people coming and going, the church was going through several changes. Our services were being held in a warehouse that was being remodeled and due to the vast openness, the acoustics were wonderful!

This particular morning, I did not feel like leading worship and had hoped that one of the other worship team members would volunteer. When I arrived, I spoke to my team member and asked if he would lead worship. He responded, "No, you can lead today."

Service began with the intercessors praying and the musicians lightly playing in the background. While they were praying, I went over in my mind what to sing. I seemed so distracted and so unconcerned with what God wanted.

Normally the intercessors would pray 25 to 30 minutes before the singers begin, but this particular morning it seemed longer. I also noticed that the praying was growing very intense. So intense, I was provoked to join in. While praying, I felt the urge to pray with great fervency and fierceness as well. So much so, it felt as if I were delivering a baby. The more I prayed from my belly, the more my spirit cried out to God for forgiveness. Forgiveness for my selfishness.

Forgiveness for not taking my responsibility seriously. Forgiveness for my poor attitude. I began to remember how there was a time I could not wait to lead worship and now that I had the opportunity to lead, I treated this privilege as if it were a burden. Shame on me!

I'm not sure how much time past, but I do know that at the conclusion of the intercessors praying, I was ready to begin singing. I had a warfare mentality and I was ready to continue in song, what the intercessors had begun. As we began to sing the atmosphere became less combative and resistant and it became easier to sing. After the fourth song, the team naturally flowed into singing and praying in the spirit. Suddenly I heard the following:

In Your Presence is where I long to be

It's where I hear Your voice

And I know Your thoughts

I know Your plan that is meant for me

In Your Presence is where I long to be

It's where I see Your face

You tell me your most intimate thoughts

In Your Presence is where I long to be

I began to sing what I heard my spirit singing. The more I sang, the more words filled my spirit. Then the praise team began singing, "Is where I long to be," while I sang:

There's healing in Your Presence

There is deliverance

And restoration

Is where I long to be

In Your Presence, in Your Presence

I long to be in Your Presence

The team continued to sing, "Is where I long to be," while I began to sing the song in the spirit. The song began to climb to a higher level and then I sang,

I love you Jesus, Oh I love you Jesus

In Your Presence, Oh Lord in Your Presence

Is where I want to be, I want to be, I want to be in Your Presence

Is where I want to be

Is where I want to be

Oh there's nothing like being in the Presence of

THE MOTIVATION, MESSAGE AND MEANING BEHIND THE MUSIC

The Almighty God, the Everlasting Father, Oh the Prince of Peace

Who gives me the peace that passes all understanding

Oh it's nothing like being in Your Presence

It's where I long to be, it's where I long to be

In Your Presence is where I long to be

There's healing

there's deliverance

there is forgiveness and restoration

Is where I want to be

As I look back and listen to the tape, it amazes me how everyone flowed so well. From that song, we flowed right into another new song. The music and the atmosphere gradually changed from intimate to militant. Greg Landfair, the head musician began to play very aggressively and I heard the words:

We're marching onto the battlefield

With a two-edged sword in our hand

We're pulling down strong-holds in the name of Jesus

We sang this song for almost 20 minutes and the song seemed to take on it's own character and sound.

Over a year later, I was going through some of the tapes in my car and found the tape from that Sunday morning, March 26, 2000. When I listened to the tape, the music and words ministered to my spirit. I played the song over and over again until I thought, "I'm going to record this song."

By this time, my husband and I were members of Life Changers International Church with Pastors Gregory and Grace Dickow. I approached the head musician, Pastor Keith Cistrunk about recording *"In Your Presence."* To my surprise, he was more than willing to assist me in any way. We agreed to meet and review the song to put together a script for the musicians and background vocals. He introduced me to Lisa Thiel who assisted on the administrative end of the project as well as her husband Doug Thiel who designed the CD cover.

Pastor Keith was so very resourceful and so much a part of bringing forth the vision, it felt as if this were his vision as well. Even though he is an authoritarian, he walks in great humility, which ministered to me greatly. He is very perceptive of people and desires to see the men and women of God walk into their divine purpose. He is the epitome of encouragement!

THE MOTIVATION, MESSAGE AND MEANING BEHIND THE MUSIC

Pastor Keith and I worked together to clean up the song and one day at rehearsal he stated that he heard the following bridge:

In Your Presence there is fullness of joy

at Your right-hand there are pleasures forever more

He also suggested that we change the word "long" to "love". With such a minor change, the song took on a whole new meaning! After three or four rehearsals, we decided that it was time to go into the studio.

The recording was wonderful; very uplifting and triumphant. Pastor Keith did a wonderful job with the background vocals and harmony. However, I felt that the song needed to be more intimate and personal. I did not hear drums in the song and I heard lighter background vocals. The more I listened to the song, the more I heard Greg Landfair's guitar. So I contacted Greg and within a couple of days, we went into the studio to lay new tracks.

One version of the song was not better than the other version, it had to do with where I was spiritually at that time.

The Meaning

When I sing, "In Your Presence," what am I saying to God? Let's take the word "Presence." Presence comes from the Greek word parousia, formed from parra' meaning "with" and ousia meaning "being"; derived from eimi meaning "to be". So parousia literally means, "a being with".[iv]

The word "Your" refers to God the Father, the Son and the Holy Spirit. So in essence, when I sing, "In Your Presence," I am referring to a being with The Father, The Son and The Holy Spirit in a place called there. There, is a place of great intimacy. In *Deuteronomy 12:11* it states, *"Then there shall be a place which the Lord your God shall choose to cause his name to dwell there."*

Earlier in chapter 1, I stated that the tabernacle of the congregation consisted of the court of the tabernacle, the holy place and the most holy. The presence of God resided in the most holy and when Jesus Christ died on the cross for our sins, rose from the dead and ascended into heaven to be with the Father, the earthly tabernacle became a heavenly tabernacle.

Now if the presence of God resides in the most holy place and also dwells within us, then the heavenly most holy place must be within us.

I find it interesting that the tabernacle of the congregation consisted of three parts; the court of the tabernacle, the holy place and the most holy.

THE MOTIVATION, MESSAGE AND MEANING BEHIND THE MUSIC

The Godhead consists of three parts; the Father, the Son and the Holy Spirit. Furthermore, the human body consists of three parts; the body, the mind and the heart. If we look at this closely we will see that the body which contains the mind and the heart represents the court of the tabernacle which contains the holy place and the most holy. The mind which is connected to the heart represents the holy place which is connected to the most holy. Finally the heart which is the dwelling place of the Lord represents the most holy place which is where the Ark of the Covenant or the Presence of God dwells.

However, in *John 15:4* it states, *"Abide in me, and I in you."* This tells me that not only does God abide or live within us, we must live within Him as well. (*Acts 17:28*) When we dwell in Him and He dwells in us, then we produce fruit and live a full prosperous life.

In *Psalms 91:1*, it states, *"He that dwelleth in the secret place of the most High shall abide under the shadow of the Almighty."* A secret is "concealed from general knowledge or view; kept hidden." So the secret place is hidden from the general knowledge or view, just as the most holy was hidden from the general congregation in the days of ancient Israel. The most holy was a secret to the rest of the congregation because only the high priest or someone of spiritual authority experienced it.

I am reminded of when I was a child in school. Often times I wondered what was in the teacher's lounge. Whenever the door opened, I would try to get a quick glance. It was a secret place because it was not open to the general student body.

There are so many levels, and levels within levels within God. In *Psalms 100:4* it states, *"Enter into his gates with thanksgiving, and into his courts with praise."* The "s" on the end of gates and courts tells me that there is more than one gate and more than one court. So this explains how everyone can exist in a different place spiritually. Some people live in the outer court, some in the holy place and some in the most holy. That is why in *Matthew 9:29* it states, "… according to your faith, be it unto you." According to where you are in God, determines your level of faith. If you currently dwell in the outercourt, your faith may not be as great as someone who dwells in the innercourt.

When we look at the phrase, "Is where I love to be," this is probably the most important part of the song. When Pastor Keith suggested changing "long" to "love", it was key. The change was important because it took the song from desiring to commune with the Father to being thankful for already being in that state. The bible says in *Matthew 5:6*, *"Blessed are they which do hunger and thirst after righteousness: for they shall be filled."* The word "righteous" means to be in right standing with God. When Jesus died for our sins, we were made righteous. (*Romans 5:19*) If we are already righteous because of the blood of the lamb, why do we desire to be something that we are. If we are seated with Him in heavenly places as it states in *Ephesians 2:6,* then it is not necessary to hope that we will get there one day. If we are already "there" then we do not "long " to be there but we "love" being there.

The Message

When I listen to, "In Your Presence," I can never play it just one time. I've noticed that when I play the song, I never hear the ending of the song. My thoughts become consumed with things that are true, honest, just, pure, and lovely. (*Philippians 4:8*)

I would love to say that since my spiritual rebirth, I have always rested in God and thought on only these things, but that would not be the truth. It was not until recently that I experienced a secret place and "I got it!" A light bulb came on and I understood what life is about and who I am and who's I am!!! Yes, I am always in His presence because He lives within me and I in Him. However, it was not until the Holy Spirit Himself revealed to me this hidden place that I understood. I did not always dwell in this particular secret place where I clearly hear the voice of God and understand.

When I first excepted Jesus Christ as my personal Lord and Savior, it was because the Holy Spirit revealed the hidden mystery of salvation to me. Once I understood that Jesus Christ loved me and died for me so that I could have everlasting life and life more abundantly, I entered into His gates. I was so very thankful and so excited as a babe in Christ! It has been over twelve years and since then I have moved from one gate to another and from one court to another. The only way I moved from one gate and court to another gate and court was because the Holy Spirit Himself revealed another mystery to me. The moment or the place in which He revealed Himself or a mystery to me was the "secret place." The place called "there." So in essence, all of God's children have been to a place called "there" because there, is the place where the Holy Spirit reveals a mystery or something that was hidden to you. When you first excepted Jesus Christ as your personal Lord and Savior, you were at a place called "there". The Holy Spirit revealed a secret or hidden place to you. Therefore, the secret place can be in the outer courts as well as the inner courts.

    The Holy Spirit is always talking to me but because of being so bombarded with distractions from television, radio, my career and even my family, many times I do not hear the still small voice. The still small voice is a subtle thought that can easily be disregarded because of distractions. But when I hear the voice and chose to get understanding, I get excited about what the Holy Spirit reveals to me! I now walk in revelation knowledge. Revelation knowledge is simply walking in understanding that has been revealed to us by the Holy Spirit. Each time we hear the Holy Spirit and seek understanding, we enter into a new gate or court within God.

    How do we get to a secret place? All you have to do is rest in God. The word rest means "to be or continue to be; remain." We simply have to be in God or continue to be in God. We remain in God by removing the distractions of this world. That is done by praying, meditating on God and God's word, and singing praises unto the Lord.

The bible says in *Ephesians 6:18, "Praying always with all prayer and supplication in the Spirit, and watching thereunto with all perseverance and supplication..."* In *Jude 1:20,* we are told to, *"build ourselves up on our most holy faith by praying in the Holy Ghost."*

We must meditate on God. David said, *"Surely I have composed and quieted my soul; like a weaned child rests against his mother, my soul is like a weaned child within me."* (*Psalms 131:3*) No matter how old my children are, there are times when each of them will sit on my lap or in my arms for me to hold them. It is a time when my love for them is being reinforced and they meditate on that moment. The same should happen with God. We can climb up into His arms, close our eyes and think about His goodness.

We must meditate on God's word. *Joshua 1:8* says, *"This book of the law shall not depart out of thy mouth; but thou shalt meditate therein day and night, that thou mayest observe to do according to all that is written therein: for then thou shalt make thy way prosperous, and then thou shalt have good success."* Many times when I hear the voice of the Lord, a small phrase or a part of a scripture will come to my spirit. I research the scriptures and through the word of God, the Holy Spirit reveals what God is trying to say. If I do not meditate and study the word of God, how will I know that what I am hearing is the voice of God and understand what God is saying.

Finally, we are to sing to the Lord. In *Colossians 3:16* it states that, *"we are to let the word of Christ dwell in us richly in all wisdom; teaching and admonishing one another in psalms and hymns and spiritual songs, singing with grace in our hearts to the Lord."*

So when you listen to *"In Your Presence,"* know that because of the blood of the Lamb you are already in the presence of God. However, God desires for us to experience and know Him in a more intimate and deeper way where we think on only those things that are true, honest, just, pure, and lovely. In order to do that, we need to block out all distractions. Once this is done, the Holy Spirit takes us "there." There is a secret place where the Holy Spirit Himself reveals something that was hidden to us. When we get understanding behind the revelation, then we enter into a new gate or court within God and in turn produce greater fruit and live a fuller prosperous life!

THE MOTIVATION, MESSAGE AND MEANING BEHIND THE MUSIC

Chapter VI – Your Glory

The Motivation

Jesus I love You

I praise and adore Your Holy name

You became a sacrifice

I have eternal life

As we sit at the right-hand of the Father

Jesus I love You

I glorify and magnify Your name

You surround me with Your love

Cover me with Your blood

And now You call me Your own

Your glory

Your glory

Your glory is revealed in me

The whole world can see Your manifested power

Being demonstrated in me

Your glory

It was September of 2001, the last month of the quarter and our fiscal year-end. It was crunch time for the entire sales force. Our last opportunity to either meet or exceed our yearly quotas. My quota for the year was $20 million and I only needed a little over a million to go. It was pretty much a guarantee that I would make achievers this year. It had been a great year for me. The company was trying to get through the many changes that we were experiencing and recover from the vast number of employees who accepted the early retirement buy-out package. I not only had to work my accounts but 5 additional accounts of a former team member who could not resist the tempting retirement package that was offered to her. One of those accounts being a "cash cow." A local county board. They had just signed a contract for over $3 million for telecommunications equipment for the new county hospital scheduled to open the following year and the commission was mine! All mine!!

For a year I had been watching a certain upscale development in my neighborhood and I prayed that God would one day give me a house in this development. I would drive up and down the streets of the development and say, "Thank you

Father for my new house." I had become a regular visiting the model. When I realized that my commission would be over $15k, my husband and I agreed that we would put that money toward a down-payment for a home. We drove over to the model in the development, which was for sale. That was not a good sign because usually the model is the last of the properties to be put up for sale. In fact, the sales associate was no longer located on premise and we drove to another development owned by the same builder. When we arrived, we talked to the sales associate about the development that I was interested in. To my surprise, he informed me that not only was the model for sale, but two spec homes as well. We asked to see the homes and drove over to the development. The model I had seen many times before, but the first house we visited, I knew was our home. When the sales associate unlocked and opened the door, all of our mouths dropped. The first floor was open and spacious and there was wall-to-wall white carpet. We immediately took off our shoes and our journey began. The sales associate did not have to sell us because the house sold itself. The children went straight to the stairs to the second floor where they began to claim what room belong to them. I remember when my husband and I saw the master suite and then the master bath and walk-in closet. What really took my breath away was the view from the master bedroom window. There was a forest preserve in the back of the home that had white-tailed deer, foxes, coyotes and other animals.

The sales associate left my husband and I alone to talk. I immediately said, "Babe, I want this house. This is our house!" He responded, "Babe, it's beautiful but where are we going to get the money?" I told my husband that if we believe the prophet, so shall we prosper. (*2 Chronicles 20:20*)

I was referring to, two separate prophetic words that I received from two prophets of God; Janet Floyd and Bishop Bernard Jordan. In 1999, while a member of New Wine Church, I received a very specific word from God through Prophetess Janet Floyd. At the very end of the prophesy she said, "I see a house that you've been talking about. I see you and your husband driving up and down the street and you saying, 'Baby, this is the kind of neighborhood I want to live in.' God said 'that He is going to give you the house that you want in the neighborhood you choose.'"

For my birthday in January of 2001, Bishop Bernard Jordan sent a cassette tape with the following prophesy, "I see that in the month of October you are going to have the eagle's eye and you're going to think with the mind of a fox. You shall be skillful in matters of real-estate and you will begin a new lifestyle."

The sales associate then took us down the street to another spec home that was much smaller. However, I was not interested because I saw the house that I wanted and I was determined to stand on God's Word and believe the prophets.

It was the last week of the month and I wanted to make sure that the contract for the new hospital was processed. After my inquiry, I became concerned because almost three weeks had gone by and the contract was not uploaded in our system. This process should take no more than a week. I contacted our contract specialist over and over again and when I finally tracked her down, she stated that our new Vice President who officially would not start his new job title until our new fiscal year, October 1, 2001 instructed her to hold the contract until October 1st. By doing so, he would begin his first fiscal quarter and year as a new Vice President with a huge contract already signed.

    I immediately called my new Vice President and asked if he instructed the contract specialist to hold the contract, and he said, "I did." I shared with him my interest in using the commission from that sale and how time was of the essence. If the contract did not upload into the system before October 1st, then I may not see the commission from the sale until December 1st. I was concerned that by that time, the house would be sold to someone else. He offered to write a letter to the builder guaranteeing that I would have a commission of $15k by December 1st in hope that the house could be held for us.

    So October came and it was a new fiscal year. I found out that I was expecting baby #6 in June of 2002, my first CD, "In Your Presence," was going to be released within a couple of weeks and my husband and I had agreed that we would deplete our savings and put a down payment on our home. On October 24, 2001, my Vice President wrote the letter as promised and with that we put almost $15k down on our home. Our closing date was scheduled for Friday, December 14, 2001. The entire family was excited and we would go by the house everyday and stretch our hands toward the house to say, "Thank you God for our beautiful home." In the morning, in the afternoon and in the evening, I would drive past my house and thank God.

November was here and my CD's had arrived. I mailed out over 1000 copies to various ministries, family members and friends. I sowed my entire first project in hope that God would reap a harvest of souls and bless me to do a full project. My pregnancy was going very well and I had began to pack in preparation of moving into our new home the following month.

The last day of November I was to receive my huge commission check and Michael and I would have the remainder of our money to close on our home. However, when payday arrived, my huge check did not arrive. I immediately called payroll to inquire. To give some background information, in October of 2000, our company was spun off from a larger global telecommunications company. Even though we were a separate company, we still shared many of the same systems and databases. In October of 2001, we truly became an independent company with our own systems and databases. With that said, change over in payroll and other areas within the company, did not go as expected. Each sales associate received their base pay but for some reason the company said that they had no way of tracking what we actually sold and therefore did not know how much our commission should be. So as a result, they gave every employee a set amount for commission and stated that a true-up would be performed at the end of December. This was called a draw check. Of course the draw check was no where near what I was expecting or needed. When I informed Michael of the situation, we immediately called the builder to inform them of the circumstances. To my surprise, the builder stated that if we did not close on the scheduled date, then we can be sued for the balance of the down payment as well as any legal fees. Not only could we be sued but we would be charged for each day after our closing date until we close.

Suddenly it felt as though the world were caving in on me and I could not breathe. Our backs were literally against the wall and time was running out. We were suppose to be out of our current home by the end of November so we asked the gentleman who purchased the home if we could stay an additional two weeks and in exchange we would give him our appliances. He agreed and we were able to stay in the house for two additional weeks.

The two weeks came and left and it was time for us to move out. My husband rented a storage space to store our furniture, clothes and personal items in and we made reservations at a local hotel. I remember the first night telling the children that we would not be in the hotel for very long. There were two full size beds for two adults and five children. We instructed our children not to make any noise because we did not know how long we would have to stay and we did not want any complaints. Benjamin, who was 8 months at the time, woke up in the middle of the night crying. Michael would fix a bottle and run down to the lobby to heat up the bottle. It seemed as though he took forever. Benjamin continued to cry louder and louder waking up the rest of the children and I feared our neighbors as well. The first couple of nights we ate out at various restaurants and when it seemed as though our situation was not going to change anytime soon, we began to buy bread and a lot of peanut butter and jelly. Michael continued to go to work and the children to school. I decided to use the remainder of my vacation so that I could concentrate on finding financial assistance. We decided to apply at other mortgage companies to get a lower rate or to get a lower down payment. Unfortunately because Michael and I filed bankruptcy in 1997, no one would approve us unless we put $30k down. However, one day I called a local mortgage company and explained our situation. The gentlemen pulled our credit report and asked several questions. He stated that since the bankruptcy, Michael and I have had excellent credit and because of that, he does not see why we can not be approved. Finally our help had come. I gathered all the necessary documentation and the gentleman stated that we should have our approval within a couple of days. We would make our scheduled closing date and not be penalized with additional fees and possibly a lawsuit.

THE MOTIVATION, MESSAGE AND MEANING BEHIND THE MUSIC

I told the children and we were all so excited. A couple of days had gone by and it was Friday, December 14, 2001, we did not hear anything in the morning and missed our closing date. I called the loan officer and left several messages. Finally, approximately 6:00 that evening while Michael, the children and I were in our car, the loan officer called my husband on his cell phone and stated that there was nothing he could do. Before Michael hung up, I knew. There was such a dead silence in the car.

We returned back to our hotel where no one said anything. That was the most depressing moment that I had ever experienced. For the first time, I was scared. I crawled in bed and curled up and cried silently to myself.

The next morning was like a new day. Michael awoke and immediately got on the telephone calling everyone that he knew to borrow the money. There were some who immediately said, "no" and some that said, "let me see what I can do and call you back later." We left detailed messages with some with no return phone call and then there were those who said yes. We called people all over the country in New Jersey, Ohio, Illinois, West Virginia, Washington DC, Kansas, Georgia and New Mexico.

Over a week had gone by and we had some commitments but it still was not enough. Then Christmas day came. Our church, Life Changers International Church has a Christmas Miracle service every year on Christmas day. We decided that we would attend and believe God for our miracle. I remember being very uplifted as soon as I walked into the sanctuary.

Pastor Dickow preached from *Philippians 4:6, "Be careful for nothing; but in every thing by prayer and supplication with thanksgiving let your petition be made known unto God."* At the end of the service, Pastor Dickow had everyone put their requests in an envelope and he would pray over each request. We went to the church office and completed a form for financial assistance. When I gave the form to one of the workers, I began to explain our situation to her in hope that we would be approved for the money. She interrupted me and said, "God knows what you have need of before you ask so believe that he has already provided it." A calmness came over me and the first time in weeks, I felt that God was truly in control.

We returned to our hotel room and my husband acted on the word that was taught that morning. He made his petition known and had all of us touch what he had written and stand in agreement with him while he prayed. Then I taught from the bible on Joseph and how he experienced many difficult times in his life but God was faithful and caused him to be successful each time.

The next morning, we continued to call friends and family members for assistance. More money came in from friends and we were approved for financial assistance from our church. Things were truly looking up. We continued to go past our house everyday and stretch our hands toward the home saying, "Thank you God for our beautiful home." The end of the month and year was approaching and we calculated that with the money that we received and our paychecks, we were only $5000 short of meeting our goal. God was truly faithful!

I called my coach to let him know that we had not moved into our house yet and I would use my vacation for the following year beginning January 1st. To my surprise, my coach stated, "You have not closed yet? We all thought that you were already in your new home." He then asked how much I needed. I told him $5000 and he said that he would call me back. When he called me back, I could not believe what had happened. My coach informed me that he had spoken to his boss, our new Vice President and they both agreed to give $2500 each. When he told me, I was in the hallway of the hotel and I just stood there and cried thanking him and thanking God.

We ended up closing on our home Thursday, January 10, 2002. The first night that we slept in our home was wonderful. I woke up around 2:00 am and walked around the house thanking God. Then I heard my spirit singing:

Jesus I love You

I praise and adore Your Holy name

You became a sacrifice

I have eternal life

As we sit at the right-hand of the Father

Jesus I love You

I glorify and magnify Your name

You surround me with Your love

Cover me with Your blood

And now You call me Your own

Your glory

Your glory

Your glory is revealed in me

The whole world can see Your manifested power

Being demonstrated in me

Your glory

The Meaning

What is the glory of God? God's glory is the manifested power of God. It is the revealed power of God and can only be manifested or revealed by the Holy Spirit. (*2 Corinthians 3:18*)
God created man in His own image and after His own likeness so that we would glorify Him. By being created in God's image and likeness, when God sees us, He actually sees Himself and His power and is therefore glorified. When we are fruitful and we multiply, then God is even more pleased because more of His power is being revealed in the earth. When God sees Himself, then He sees His power. He sees His Glory. He sees His spoken Word going forth. In fact in *Isaiah 43:7* it says, *"Everyone who is called by My name, Whom I have created for My glory; I have formed him, yes, I have made him."*
That is why praise and worship of God is so important. When we sing, "I love You Lord, Jesus you are everything to me, You are Jehovah Jireh, The Lord who provides, Jehovah Shammah, The Lord is present, Jehovah Rophe, The Lord who heals," we are simply reflecting what God has already spoken into existence. The bible says, *"But thou art holy, O thou that inhabitest the praises of Israel."* (*Psalms 22:3*) When you look up the word "inhabit," you will see that it means to dwell or to fill. To fill, means to supply or provide to the fullest extent. So if God inhabits or fills the praises of His people, then He supplies or provides to the

fullest extent, in the praises of His people. When we praise God, that is where we see healing, deliverance, restoration, creative ideas and witty inventions. That is where He supplies and provides for us.

We can not praise our way into His presence but we can praise our way into deliverance, restoration, healing, financial freedom and prosperity. You may ask, but if God lives within us then do we not already have those things? Yes, but they have to be acknowledged. To acknowledge something or someone, means "to express thanks or gratitude for." And we already know that we are to pray with thanksgiving to God. (*Philippians 4:6*) When we acknowledge the Word of God with a heart of thanksgiving, by either singing or speaking the Word, then that is when the Holy Spirit reveals God's power and we see the miraculous and the supernatural. We see power that goes beyond natural forces.

The day we accepted Jesus Christ as our personal Lord and Savior, God's power was revealed. Even then we had to call out the name of Jesus. We had to acknowledge and validate that Jesus exists. In doing so, we are saved. (*Acts 2:21*) When we speak or sing the Word of God, it goes forth from our mouths and it can not return to us void, but it shall accomplish whatever we please, and it shall prosper. (*Isaiah 55:11*)

Even God Himself had to speak the Word in order for His power to be manifested. In *Genesis 1:3*, "*And God said, Let there be light: and there was light."* In order for God to have created the world, man and every living thing, He had to speak it first. Because God is not a man that He should lie, once He speaks His Word, that which He has spoken is already done. (*Number 23:19*)

When we speak the Word of God, be assured that it will come to pass. Some words manifest quicker and easier than other words. But we should not be discouraged when we do not see immediately what we have spoken. To be discouraged means to be deprived of hope or to become hopeless. If we become hopeless, then we become faithless and this is not the perfect will of God. The just are to live by faith. (*Habakkuk 2:4*)

In *Proverbs 18:21*, it says, *"Death and life are in the power of the tongue: and they that love it shall eat the fruit thereof."* In other words, we can build up or tear down simply with what we say. If the Word of God dwells within us then we should always build up. But if the Word is not in us or we choose not to listen to the Word within us, then we tear down and we are no longer reflecting or glorifying God. When we do not reflect God, then we are in sin.

Sin is failing to reflect God. We fail to reflect God when we desire things that are not of God. In *Romans 3:23* it says, *"For all have sinned and come short of the glory of God."* Short of, means "less than or other than." So in other words, we all have reflected less than or something other than God. But the good news is that when we reflect anything less than God and we fall, we can get right back up!   For a just man falls seven times, and rises up again. (*Proverbs 24:16*)

The Message

When I sing, *"Your Glory,"* I hear the glory of God. The manifested power of God. The Holy Spirit can only reveal the glory of God when we sing or speak the Word of God.

For me, I desired a home in a particular area. Long before I new the home existed, the Holy Spirit revealed the home to His prophets. (*Amos 3:7*) The prophets spoke the home into existence. (*2 Corinthians 13:1*) I believed what the prophets told me and confessed the word with my mouth by faith. When the spoken words were manifested by the Holy Spirit, then God was glorified and I received that which was spoken.

We were created to glorify God. We were created to reflect His image and His likeness. We were created to reflect His power which is His spoken Word. Many times that means that we have to experience tribulation. Tribulation is "an experience that tests one's endurance, patience or faith." But if we hold fast the profession of our faith without wavering, (*Hebrews 10:3*) then we will receive that which has been spoken.

Tribulation is good for us. In *Romans 5:3* it says, *"...but we glory in tribulations also: knowing that tribulation worketh patience."* In other words, the power of God is manifested or revealed when our endurance, faith or patience is tested but in that testing, our endurance, faith or patience is brought out or strengthened. Being patient is acceptable to God. *"...if, when ye do well, and suffer for it, ye take it patiently, this is acceptable with God. For even hereunto were ye called: because Christ also suffered for us, leaving us an example, that ye should follow his steps."* (*2 Peter 2:20-21*) So when we feel that we are being treated unfairly, we are to still be patient, just as Jesus was.

Trials and Tribulations are not "of the devil." Many times we give the devil more credit than he deserves. The bible says that we are to submit ourselves to God, resist the devil, and he will flee from us. (*James 4:7*) If we resist the devil and he flees, how can we blame the devil? We should know that we are being set up to be blessed so that God is glorified in the earth. Therefore, we should not give the credit to the devil but we should sing and speak the Word of God with thanksgiving. We have to remember that life and death are in the tongue and we can either build up or tear down what God is doing.

Now I'm not saying that during the tribulation period, the devil will not try to deceive you and tell you something other than what God said. Believe me, during that time, I had all kinds of thoughts going through my mind. But I had to cast down those thoughts immediately. Many times I was successful and then there were some times when I was not successful and stumbled but I repented and got right back up!

Chapter VII – Ask Of Me

The Motivation

You are my children

I am Your Father

Ask of Me and I will give it to thee

Ask of Me

Ask of Me

I will make the nations your inheritance

Ask of Me

Ask of Me

I will make the ends of the earth your possession

Most of the songs that God has given me, I remember vividly where I was and what I was doing but this song is not the case. Over the years, God has given me so many songs that I was forced to create a song book. *"Ask Of Me"* was included in my book but unfortunately, I did not record any background information.

During the year of 2000, I recorded a handful of songs on cassette tape and gave to Greg Landfair. They were songs that I would possibly include on my first project. *"Ask of Me,"* was included on the tape and when I spoke to Greg about the project, he stated that he wanted to begin with this song and the reasoning behind it.

That conversation was over three years ago and I did not remember until I sat down one day to put together the songs for this project. When I remembered what Greg and I talked about, I decided to include this song on the project.

The Meaning

What is a father? A father is the begetter of a child, a male parent. A father loves, directs, protects and provides for a child. A father carries great responsibility and honor as well. It is by no accident that the first word for a baby, often times is "dada." In fact the first sound that a baby makes is often "ab." Are they trying to say abba?

Abba means father and is found in the New Testament. In *Romans 8:15* it says, *"For ye have not received the spirit of bondage again to fear; but ye have received the Spirit of adoption, whereby we cry, Abba, Father."* In other words, because God is our father, we can come to Him for whatever we may need. We do not need to be afraid, because God is love. (*1 John 4:8*) There is no fear in love; but perfect love cast out fear. (*1 John 4:18*) Fear is forced out or expelled for His children. In fact, God loves us so much that he sent His Son, Jesus Christ, to the earth to be a sacrifice and redeem us from sin. (*John 3:16*) That is true love and greater love hath no man than this. (*John 15:13*)

God the Father guides His children. (*Exodus 15:13*) To guide means to show the way by leading, directing, or advising. God lead the way for the children of Israel in a pillar of a cloud by day, and a pillar of fire by night, to give them light to go by day and night. (*Exodus 13:21*) And He directed or gave them authoritative instructions (the Ten Commandments) to meet the needs of each individual in a loving and responsible manner.

(*Exodus 20:1-17*) In *1 Thessalonians 2:11* it says that the father exhorts, encourages and implores. To exhort means to urge the proper course of conduct. To encourage means to breath courage into you and train you for the future and to implore means charge or advise.

God protects His children. *Psalms 85:2* says, "*Thou hast forgiven the iniquity of thy people, thou hast covered all their sin.*" And in *Psalms 3:1-7*, the people rose up against the Psalmist to harm him and even said that God would not help him but God rose to inflict a blow upon their cheek bone and broke their teeth. Ouch!

God provides for His children. (*Genesis 22:8-14*) *Philippians 4:19* says my God shall supply all my need according to His riches in glory by Christ Jesus. All we have to do is ask Him humbly or earnestly with thanksgiving. It is wonderful to know that what ever we ask, will be given to us! (*Matthew 7:7*) In fact *Matthew 6:8* tells us that our Father knows what we need before we even ask Him. The Father wants to bless us. In *Matthew 7:11* it says, "*If ye then, being evil, know how to give good gifts unto your children, how much more shall your Father which is in heaven give good things to them that ask him?*" In other words, if the earthly father who has evil in his heart desires to bless his children, then imagine how our Heavenly Father wants to bless us when we ask him.

Fatherhood is a huge responsibility because the father must discipline in love. To discipline a child means to train a child according to a set of rules or methods, to produce a specific character or pattern of behavior. A father must train up a child in the way he should go because then when he is old, he will not depart. (*Proverbs 22:6*) It means teaching the Word of God by example to a child, to produce an adult that reflects God's character and God's behavior. In instances where God's character and God's behavior are not being exhibited, the father is to use the rod of correction to drive far away the foolishness that is bound in the child's heart. (*Proverbs 22:15*) The bible says that fathers are not to withhold correction from a child (*Proverbs 23:13*) because it causes reverence and respect for the father. However, fathers are not to beat the child to the point of causing violent and vindictive behavior. (*Ephesians 6:4*)

Because we give reverence to our earthly fathers when they correct us, then we should give even greater reverence to God the Father. (*Hebrews 12:9*) When we give reverence, we give honor and adoration. God said that children are to honor their fathers and by doing so, they will have a long life. (*Exodus 20:12*) Honoring fathers must have been important to God because He made this the first commandment.

The Message

When I sing, *"Ask Of Me,"* I hear God the Father actually saying, *"You are my child and I have begotten you so ask of me and I will give you the nations for your inheritance and the ends of the earth for your possession."* (*Psalms 2:7-8*) This was the promise that God gave to Abraham who was known as being the father of faith and the father of nations.

Abraham means "father of a crowd or multitude." God changed Abraham's name from Abram meaning "father is high or exalted," to Abraham when he was 99 years old. During this time, God reaffirmed His promise to Abraham that He would be a father of many nations and He would make him exceedingly fruitful where even kings will come from him. (*Genesis 17:5-9*) However, when Abraham was 86 years old, Sarah his wife became discouraged because she was still barren. She then proposed to substitute her Egyptian maidservant Hagar so that she might have a child by her. Abraham consented and Ishmael was born. (*Genesis 16:3-16*) But God was faithful and when Abraham was 100 years old and Sarah was 90 years old, they had a son and named him Isaac.

Approximately 20 years later, Abraham's faith was tested. God told Abraham to take Isaac to Mount Moriah to build an altar to sacrifice his son Isaac. Abraham was obedient and just as he was about to offer Isaac as a sacrifice, God intervened

THE MOTIVATION, MESSAGE AND MEANING BEHIND THE MUSIC

and provided a ram as substitute for Isaac. Because Abraham was willing to sacrifice his son that he had waited so very long for and obeyed God, God reinforced His covenant with Abraham. (*Genesis 22:1-18*) That is why Abraham is called the father of faith.

Sarah died at the age of 127. Later Abraham married a woman named Keturah and had six additional sons. God fulfilled His prophetic utterance, "A father of a crowd of nations I will make you." Abraham was the father of the Israelites, Ishmaelites and Edomites but also Medanites, Midianites and others. (*Genesis 25:1-2; 1 Chronicles 1:28-34*) Abraham and Sarah had Isaac, Isaac married Abraham's grandniece Rebekah and together they had Esau and Jacob. Jacob married Leah, Laban's daughter who gave birth to Judah. It was from the tribe of Judah that Jesus Christ was born and in doing so the promise was fulfilled. The promise, "*ask of me and I will give you the nations for your inheritance and the ends of the earth for your possession.*" (*Psalms 2:7-8*)

Because Jesus Christ is the true seed of Abraham and because we are joint heirs with Jesus Christ, we too are the seed of Abraham by faith and by faith receive the promise that God made to Abraham. The nations are our inheritance and the ends of the earth are our possession!

When I sing, "*Ask Of Me*," I also think of my earthly father, George J. Watkins Jr. My father is a great man. He is great because he trained me up in the way that I should go so that I could be successful in life. My father is not a deeply religious man but he knows God. You may not see him shouting and giving Barak praise but that does not mean that he loves God any less.

The morals and ideals that I hold so highly are because of my father. He taught me the importance of a strong work ethic and the benefits of hard work. He taught me to acquire as much knowledge as possible because knowledge is power. He taught me to respect my elders and to say yes sir and thank you ma'am.

He is a very private man but at the same time a compassionate man who cares deeply for his family. He is a funny man and when he laughs at his own jokes, his laughter is contagious and causes me to laugh. He is a distinguished and established man.

My father is the most intelligent person I know. He is very wise and whenever I talk to him, I learn something new and beneficial. He can have any type of conversation with the best of them. He has four degrees and even graduated from Harvard University. He has traveled all over the world and I love to hear of his experiences in other countries. He has lived a life of poverty and he has been a millionaire. He is a strong man and often the one the family will look to for strength and support.

My father is a teacher, husband, friend, roll model, mentor, entrepreneur and a natural born leader. Those who know him often tell me how much they respect my father. What I love most about my father is that he is not afraid to experience life. He never considers giving up as an option and he is able to stay focused regardless of the distractions. Every wind or doctrine does not move him.

Finally, my father is a great man because all that he has instilled in me, is being passed on to his grandchildren and some day his great-grandchildren!

I love you daddy!!!

THE MOTIVATION, MESSAGE AND MEANING BEHIND THE MUSIC

Chapter VIII – Beauty For Ashes

The Motivation

The day of your deliverance

Has finally come

To comfort the broken-hearted

To liberate the captive ones

To open the eyes of the blind

To heal the afflicted mind

The day of your deliverance

Has finally come

The Lord is giving Beauty For Ashes

Joy instead of mourning

Praise for heaviness your deliverance has come

In 1993, Bishop Brian Keith Williams asked if I would write a song for his message, "Shoulder

To Shoulder." I wrote the song, we recorded a copy to accompany Bishop's message for a conference in Tulsa, Oklahoma, hosted by Bishop Carlton Pearson.

In 1994, while talking to Evangelist Freeman of New Life Ministries in New Jersey, she stated that she attended the 1993 Azusa conference and she saw my pastor. I told her that I wrote the song for his message, "Shoulder To Shoulder." She then asked if I would write the theme song for her conference, "Beauty For Ashes." She told me that the conference would be held in Atlanta, Georgia and was based on *Isaiah 61:3*. The guest ministers were Pastor Jefferson and Prophetess Debra Edwards of Freedom Christian Center in Kansas City, Missouri.

Since my spiritual rebirth, Evangelist Freeman has encouraged me through the word of God. I would call her during my mountain-top seasons as well as my valley-low seasons and I would always hang up the phone refreshed and rejuvenated. Not only is she an evangelist, but a prophet as well and she spoke the Word of the Lord every time with great accuracy into my life. In fact, she is responsible for my relationship with Bishop Bernard Jordan. When we talked, she always spoke of her pastor and his ministry. Then one day when she prophesied to me, she stated that I needed to get in touch with her pastor, Bishop Jordan because he had a word for me. My life has not been the same since!!!

The Meaning

What is salvation? Salvation derived from the Late Latin word salvti, salvtin, from salvtus, past participle of salvre, which means "to save." In general, salvation means "preservation or deliverance from destruction, difficulty, or evil." In other words, being saved from illness, starvation, oppression, ignorance, calamity and death.

The children of Israel experienced all of this and more while living in Egypt. To give some background information, God made a covenant with Abraham in *Genesis 17:5-9* and told Abraham that he would be the father of many nations. To assure Abraham that the promise would come to past, God told Abraham that his seed would become strangers in a land that was not theirs and his seed would serve them and be afflicted for 400 years. (*Genesis 15:13*)

The second meaning of salvation is "deliverance from the power or penalty of sin; redemption." In the beginning, God created the earth and everything in it as well as man. God named the man Adam and from his rib he created a partner for Adam and named her Eve. (*Genesis 2:22*) Adam and Eve lived in the Garden of Eden which contained every tree that was good for food. The garden also contained the tree of life as well as the tree of knowledge of good and evil. (*Genesis 2:9*)

God told Adam that he could eat of any tree in the garden except for the tree of knowledge of good and evil. If he ate from the tree then he would die. (*Genesis 2:17*) Well one day satan came along in the form a serpent and told Eve that if she ate from the tree of knowledge of good and evil, that she would not die but she would be like God. Satan is a deceiver and he deceived Eve to make her think that she was not already like God. But she was like God. In *Genesis 1:26* God said, *"Let Us make man in Our image, after Our likeness..."*

Adam and Eve ate of the tree and their eyes were opened. (*Genesis 3:6-7*) Adam and Eve disobeyed God and as a result were removed from the presence of God, the Garden of Eden and were cursed. The curse consisted of:

- A woman will experience great pain during childbirth

- The husband will rule over his wife

- The land will be difficult to farm for food

- Man will die and return back to the dust from which he came

Man could no longer have a personal relationship with God. He would not have eternal life and he would now have to work tirelessly for food. This was not what God had intended when He created us. Because of Adam and Eve's disobedience, they were no longer in the image and after the likeness of God. Therefore, they were in sin. They no longer reflected the image and likeness of God.

When we were born into the earth, we were sinners because of Adam and Eve's disobedience. It is our nature from birth to have evil in our hearts. That is why parents are to train their children because we come in this world wanting to do wrong. It is our nature. Nature is the fundamental character or disposition of a person.

Living this way was displeasing to God. When He created us, His intentions were for us to have dominion and power over everything and to live freely forever. In order for man to get back to the way God intended him to live, man needed deliverance from the power and penalty of sin. Man needed salvation.

In order to bring salvation to mankind, God had to send someone who was a God and someone who was a man at the same time. He had to be enough God to deliver us from sin and enough man to fill our infirmities. In *Isaiah 53:5* it says that he was wounded for our transgressions and bruised for our iniquities.

Therefore, His Son, Jesus Christ who is God, was born into the earth. In *2 Corinthians 5:21* it says, *"For he hath made him to be sin for us, who knew no sin; that we might be made the righteousness of God in him."* In other words, God sent His Son Jesus Christ, who was actually God in the flesh on earth, who knew no sin, to restore mankind back in right standing with God. To take on the sin of Adam and Eve so that we can be righteous and once again glorify God. We would then live freely and have everlasting life.

So Jesus was born into the earth. While in the earth he had 12 disciples that he taught and trained in the things of God. They watched him heal the sick, deliver those possessed by satan and most of all fulfill the words of the book written by the prophet Isaiah.

In *Luke 4:16-22*, Jesus had gone into the synagogue on the Sabbath day in Nazareth and stood up to read the book of the prophet Isaiah which said, *"The Spirit of the Lord is upon me, because he hath anointed me to preach the gospel to the poor; he hath sent me to heal the brokenhearted, to preach deliverance to the captives, and recovering of sight to the blind, to set at liberty them that are bruised, to preach the acceptable year of the Lord."* Jesus sat down and then said, *"This day is this scripture fulfilled in your ears."* Jesus was saying, "Your deliverance is here! Your salvation is here!" "I am the one that the prophet Isaiah spoke of." "I have come that you have life and have life more abundantly!" (*John 10:10*)

The Message

When I sing, *"Beauty For Ashes,"* I think of the price that Jesus Christ paid for us to have everlasting life. When Jesus died, our sins died with Him. In *Psalms 103:12* it says, *"As far as the east is from the west, so far has He removed our transgressions from us."* Transgressions are "offenses, crimes, or sins." God will never remember our sins because the east and west will never meet. God separates us from our sins and He does not remember it. God forgives and forgets, that is true forgiveness.

2 Corinthians 5:17 says, *"Therefore if any man be in Christ, he is a new creature: old things are passed away; behold, all things are become new."* When Christ was buried, our old nature was buried and we took on the nature or reflection of God. So the things that we used to say and do, we do not say and do anymore. Instead we desire the things of God. Of course the complete transformation does not happen over night because there is a process. Our minds have to be renewed. In *Romans 12:2* it says, *"And be not conformed to this world: but be ye transformed by the renewing of your mind, that ye may prove what is that good, and acceptable, and perfect, will of God."*

When Jesus rose from the dead and ascended into heaven, we too ascended and sit with the Father. *Romans 8:17* says, *"And if children, then heirs; heirs of God, and joint-heirs with Christ..."*

As joint-heirs with Christ Jesus, we are the head and not the tail, above only and not beneath. (*Deuteronomy 28:13*) We are the righteousness of God and therefore we are surrounded with favor as a shield. (*Psalms 5:12*)

As a result of salvation, the broken-hearted have been comforted. Jesus said in *John 14:26* that the Father will send in the name of Jesus, the Comforter, which is the Holy Ghost to teach us all things and bring all things to our remembrance. To comfort means "to make strong; to invigorate; to fortify; to corroborate." How will the Holy Spirit make us strong when our hearts have been broken? He will bring to remembrance the Word of God and remind us of what God said. The Word being Christ Jesus, will make us strong. *"I can do all things through Christ which strengtheneth me."* (*Philippians 4:13*)

Salvation liberated the captive ones. *2 Corinthians 3:17* says, *"Now the Lord is that Spirit: and where the Spirit of the Lord is, there is liberty."* Wherever Jesus Christ is, there is freedom. Jesus made us free and we are free indeed. (*John 8:36*) Indeed means "Without a doubt; certainly."

Salvation opened the eyes of the blind. To be blind means that you are "unable or unwilling to perceive or understand." This could be physical or spiritual blindness. *Proverbs 4:7* tells us that *"Wisdom is the principal thing; therefore get wisdom: and with all thy getting get understanding."* In other words, we can have all the degrees in the world and the best education that money can buy, but if we do not know Jesus Christ as our personal Lord and Savior, and understand that He died so that we may live, then we are blind. And if we do know Jesus as our personal Lord and Savior or we do not apply the Word of God to our daily lives and stand on God's word in the good times as well as the testing times, then we are blind. In *2 Peter 1:5-9* Peter tells us that we are to add virtue, knowledge, self-control, perseverance, godliness, brotherly kindness and love to our daily actions and we will be fruitful in the knowledge of Jesus Christ. If we do not add these things, then we are blind and we have forgotten that we were cleansed from our old sins.

Salvation healed the afflicted mind. To be afflicted means "to be mentally or physically unfit." For God has not given us the spirit of fear; but of power, and of love, and of a sound mind. (*2 Timothy 1:7*) A sound mind is having a firm basis. It is a mind that is unshakable. The enemy can not torment an unshakable mind because the mind is saturated with The Word and when the enemy comes to plant a subtle thought, it is cast down by the Word.

Salvation gave us beauty for ashes. Ashes is the result of being burned or the remains of the dead. To be dead means "having lost life and no longer alive." But beauty means "the quality that gives pleasure to the mind or senses." So all the areas of our life that were dead and did not glorify God are not only alive through the blood of Jesus Christ, but are made beautiful in the sight of God.

Salvation gave us joy for mourning. God does not want us to live our lives in deep regret but He wants his joy to be in us so that our joy will be full. (*John 15:11*) Joy in the Holy Ghost is the kingdom of God (*Romans 14:17*)

Finally, salvation gave the garment of praise for the spirit of heaviness. Heaviness is "burdensome or oppressive to the spirit." Jesus said in *Matthew 11:29* *"Take my yoke upon you, and learn of me." "For my yoke is easy, and my burden is light."* (*Matthew 11:30*) A yoke is "a crossbar with two U-shaped pieces that encircle the necks of a pair of oxen or other draft animals working together." It allows both animals to share the load or burden. In other words, Jesus is saying that we do not have to carry the load or burden ourselves. If we are yoked with him then our lives will be much lighter and easier, therefore allowing us to extol or exalt God. Being yoked to Jesus allows us to do what we were created to do, glorify God!

THE MOTIVATION, MESSAGE AND MEANING BEHIND THE MUSIC

Chapter IX – Now Is The Time

The Motivation

In these last days

You can clearly see

that everything in God's prophesy

is coming to past

We can no longer

Have the question of knowing

Of Jesus' coming

And the end of the world

Many have a form of Godliness

But deny the power thereof

You hear of war and rumors of war

Kingdom against kingdom

Chapter IX

Now is the time

For the people of the Lord

To go to all the nations and be a witness to the world

Now is the time

To tell everyone of a Great Man

Who came to die for our sins that we may have life everlasting

Now Is The Time

There are earthquakes in various places

Famine in foreign lands

People dying of so many diseases

These are the signs that we're nearing the end

It was June of 1996 and I had to get to New Jersey in time so that I could minister. I had been asked once again by Evangelist Glenda Freeman to write the theme song for their conference, "Now Is The Time." The guest speakers were Prophetess Connie Williams, Prophetess Debra Edwards, Bishop Martin and Minister Ruth Woodford.

When Prophetess Freeman asked me to write the theme song, initially I did not hear anything in my spirit and even became concerned.

THE MOTIVATION, MESSAGE AND MEANING BEHIND THE MUSIC

Finally after praying and asking God for the song, four weeks later I heard, "Now Is The Time." I decided to drive to the conference from Columbus, Ohio. I practiced the entire time, singing the song over and over again for over eight hours. Finally I arrived and when it was time for me to minister, the God-in-me ministered with great might and power!!!

The Meaning

What is the Gospel of Jesus Christ? Gospel is from the Greek word euaggelion meaning "good news." It is the good news of the life, death, and resurrection of Jesus Christ and his teachings. Jesus taught on the kingdom of God and salvation by faith in Him. The gospel is good news because it offers freedom, hope, peace and eternal life with God.

The Gospel of Jesus Christ was first declared by God when he told Abraham, *"In thee shall all nations be blessed."* (*Galatians 3:8*) From the previous chapter we learned that Jesus Christ was from the line of the tribe of Judah which traced back to Abraham and Sarah. We also learned that the prophet Isaiah spoke of Jesus Christ in *Isaiah 61:1-3* and in *Luke 4:21*, Jesus made the statement, *"This day is this scripture fulfilled in your ears*, because He was the deliverer that the prophet Isaiah wrote about.

God sent the angel Gabriel to the city of Galilee where a young woman named Mary lived and told her that she was favored of the Lord and would bring forth a son and would call Him Jesus. He will be great and He will have a throne in a kingdom that has no end. (*Luke 1:26-33*)

John the Baptist preached the good news of Jesus saying, *"Repent ye: for the kingdom of heaven is at hand."* (*Matthew 3:2*) And in *Matthew 4:17* Jesus preached, *"Repent: for the kingdom of heaven is at hand."*

THE MOTIVATION, MESSAGE AND MEANING BEHIND THE MUSIC

What does it mean to repent? Repent means "to turn away from sin." *1 John 1:9* says, *"If we confess our sins, he is faithful and just to forgive us our sins, and to cleanse us from all unrighteousness."* When we sin, we do not glorify God but we glorify the devil. He was the first to sin and as a result of sin, Jesus Christ was born into the earth to destroy sin. (*1 John 3:8*) The bible says that sinners will have their part in the lake that burns with fire and brimstone. Sinners are people who are fearful, unbelievers, abominable, murderers, whoremongers, sorcerers, idolaters and all liars. (*Revelation 21:8*) *1 Corinthians 6:9-10* says, *"neither fornicators, nor idolaters, nor adulterers, nor effeminate, nor abusers of themselves with mankind, nor thieves, nor covetous, nor drunkards, nor revilers, nor extortioners, shall inherit the kingdom of God."* *Mark 7:22* says, *"thefts, covetousness, wickedness, deceit, lasciviousness, an evil eye, blasphemy, pride, foolishness."* So if you are someone who is cowardly and doubts or questions the Word of God, does not believe in Jesus Christ, is hateful, has unlawfully killed someone, associates with or pays for sexual relations with prostitutes or a prostitute, uses supernatural powers over others through the assistance of evil spirits or practices witchcraft, worships other gods, lies, is unmarried and has sexual intercourse, is married and has sexual intercourse with someone other than your spouse, is a man and has qualities or characteristics more often associated with women than men, is a woman and has qualities or characteristics more often associated with men than women, steals, desires the possessions of another, habitually drinks, attacks with abusive language, obtains from another by coercion or intimidation, causes others to believe what is not true or you mislead others, gives to or expresses lust, has an evil eye, speaks evil of God or claims for oneself the attributes and rights of God, is arrogant or performs disdainful conduct or treatment, or lacks or exhibits a lack of good sense or judgment then you will not inherit the kingdom of God unless you repent.

The only sin that God will not forgive is blasphemy against the Holy Ghost.(*Matthew 12:31*) Anyone who refuses to acknowledge God's power in Christ will not be forgiven because their heart is hard and they will never ask for forgiveness.

What is the kingdom of God? First let us understand what a kingdom is. A kingdom is "a realm or sphere in which one thing is dominant." *In Mark 1:15*, Jesus says, *"The time is fulfilled, and the kingdom of God is at hand. Repent, and believe in the gospel."* Jesus was saying that He is the kingdom of God on earth. Jesus is the realm or sphere in which God dominates. That is why in *John 14:9* Jesus says, "*he that hath seen me hath seen the Father*," because God is Jesus. And if you have seen Jesus, then you have seen God and His kingdom.

When Jesus sent out the seventy messengers, He instructed them to heal the sick where they were accepted and to say, *"The kingdom of God is come nigh unto you."* Why did they say, "is come nigh unto you" instead of "is at hand?" Because they were not Jesus Christ, the kingdom of God but they were letting them know that Jesus Christ is near. He will be coming this way and He told us to come and He would be here soon. (*Luke 10:1*)

Who can enter into the Kingdom of God? *Matthew 7:21* says, "*Not every one that saith unto me, Lord, Lord, shall enter into the kingdom of heaven; but he that doeth the will of my Father which is in heaven.*" What is God's will? In *Matthew 6:10* it says, "Thy *kingdom come, Thy will be done in earth as it is in heaven.*" In other words, God's will is that He be glorified in the earth like He is glorified in heaven. In order for that to occur, God has to live within us. He has to abide in us and we have to abide in Him or His Word. (*John 15:7*)

Jesus taught on salvation by faith. Remember that in the previous chapter, I stated that salvation is "deliverance from the power or penalty of sin." Jesus taught that we are delivered from the power or penalty of sin by faith. If faith is the substance of things hoped for, the evidence of things not seen, (*Hebrews 11:1*) then our deliverance begins with a belief that initially we may not see. But if we continue to call those things that be not as though they were, (*Romans 4:17*) that which we have called will eventually be seen. In fact *Romans 14:23* tells us that whatever is not done in faith is sin. Our salvation begins with believing in a God that we can not see but if we do not have faith then we do not believe in Jesus Christ.

The Message

When I sing, *"Now Is The Time"* I think about the second coming of Jesus Christ. In *Matthew 24:3-14*, the disciples ask how they will know of Jesus' coming and the end of the age. Jesus tells them that many will come in His name, there will be wars and rumors of wars, nation against nation and kingdom against kingdom, famines, pestilence and earthquakes in various places. Jesus said not to be troubled because all these things must come to pass and all these things are the beginning of sorrows but the end is not yet. He goes on to say that, they will deliver believers up to tribulation and kill us and we will be hated by all nations for His name' sake, many will be offended, will betray one another and hate one another, many false prophets will rise up and deceive many, because lawlessness will abound, the love of many will grow cold. With all of this going on, the believers who endure until the end will be saved. Finally when the gospel of the kingdom is preached to all the world as a witness to all the nations, then the end will come.

Now is the time that we need to take heed more than ever to the teachings of Jesus Christ. We are truly living in the last days and the signs are all around us. Many have come already in the name of Jesus like Jim Jones who formed Jonestown and over 900 people including 276 children were murdered or committed suicide. And David Koresh who claimed he was head of the biblical House of David.

We hear of war and rumors of war everyday. We are being bombarded daily with rumors of terrorists attacks and homeland security to an ever increasing number of young suicide bombers. There are wars or rumors of war between the United States of America and Iraq, North Korea and the United States, there are airfare wars, Arab-Israeli wars, video game wars, holy war and urban warfare.

We hear of pestilence or fatal diseases all the time such as AIDs, SARs, Mad Cow Disease and now there is a new strain of the flu that is killing children.

We hear of earthquakes in various places such as Iran (2003), Turkey (2003), China (2003), Wyoming (2003), California (2003), Afghanistan (2002), India (2001), Taiwan (1999), Turkey (1999), and Colombia (1999).

We may not see much of this in the United States but many believers in other countries are being harassed, imprisoned and even killed for preaching and teaching the gospel of the kingdom of God in such places as China, Saudi Arabia and Egypt.

Now is definitely the time to tell everyone, of the gospel of Jesus Christ; Jesus was born in the earth and took on the sins of man where He suffered, died and was buried but on the third day He rose from the dead and ascended into heaven and is seated at the right-hand of the Father. We His people being forgiven of our sins, wait for His return where He will descend from heaven with a shout, with the voice of an archangel, and with the trumpet of God. And the dead in Christ will rise first. Then we who are alive and remain shall be caught up together with them in the clouds to meet the Lord in the air. And we will be with the Lord forever and ever.

I would like to encourage you right now if you do not already know Jesus Christ as your personal Lord and Savior then the good news is you still have time! The bible says, if we confess with our mouth the Lord Jesus, and believe in our heart that God has raised him from the dead, we shall be saved. (*Romans 10:9*)

It is that simple, just repeat the following and believe that it is true and you will have everlasting life:

> *"Dear Jesus, I repent of my sins and I ask for your forgiveness. I believe that your Father raised you from the dead and I commit my life to you right now. Thank you Jesus for saving me. Holy Spirit thank you from this day forward for guiding me into all truth as I study Your word. In the name of Jesus, Amen."*

Now if you just said this prayer, then you are saved! The bible says that there is greater joy in heaven for one sinner that repents than over ninety and nine people who do not need to repent. I would like to encourage you to do the following:

THE MOTIVATION, MESSAGE AND MEANING BEHIND THE MUSIC

- Go and tell someone of your rebirth. When Jesus delivered the man with the unclean spirit, he told him to go home to his friends, and tell them the great things the Lord has done for him. (*Mark 5:19*)

- Pray. We are to be careful for nothing; but in every thing by prayer and supplication with thanksgiving let our requests be made known unto God. (*Philippians 4:6*)

- Study the bible. We are to study to show ourselves approved unto God. (*2 Timothy 2:15*)

- Join a church and get connected. Joining a local assembly that teaches sound doctrine will allow you to grow spiritually. (*Ephesians 4:16*)

Finally, I would like to say welcome to the family of God! God loves you and He will never leave nor forsake you. Even when you have blown it so bad, He will still love you. Now that you are a child of God, your life will never be the same so GET READY!

THE MOTIVATION, MESSAGE AND MEANING BEHIND THE MUSIC

Chapter X – Zion

The Motivation

Can you hear Zion calling

Can you hear Zion calling

Can you hear Zion calling you to a higher place of praise

I can hear Zion calling

I can hear Zion calling

I can hear Zion calling me to a higher place of praise

"*Zion*" is another song that I do not remember where I was or what I was doing at the time when I received the song. I do remember singing and teaching the song to my dear friend Angela Bosman. My earliest memory is sometime after 1992.

However, the second verse was added when I went into the studio to record the song. While recording the song, I felt that it was important to acknowledge that I do hear Zion calling me to a higher place of praise. While singing the second verse, I then heard the ending, "praise."

By this being the last song on the project. I wanted the ending to be powerful and uplifting, so that the song leaves you energized and ready to take your praise and relationship with God to a new level!

The Meaning

What is the meaning of Zion? Is it the city of David, the place of God's dwelling or the heavenly Jerusalem? In *1 Kings 8:1* it says, *"Then Solomon assembled the elders of Israel... that they might bring up the ark of the covenant of the Lord out of the city of David, which is Zion.* And in *1 Chronicles 11:5* it says, *"And the inhabitants of Jebus said to David, Thou shalt not come hither. Nevertheless David took the castle of Zion, which is the city of David.*

When David was 30 years old, the people of Hebron anointed David king over Israel. David and his men traveled from Hebron to Jerusalem where the Jebusites occupied the land. The Jebusites boasted of their security behind the impregnable walls, which were considered the stronghold of Zion. However, David surprised them by entering through the watershaft and took the land and called it the City of David. David then established his royal residence there. (*2 Samuel 5:6-12*)

Later in *2 Samuel 6:17*, David brought the Ark of the Lord which was the presence of God into the City of David where it remained until King Solomon moved it to Mount Moriah. Then all of Jerusalem was called Zion. (*1 Kings 8:1*) Because the Ark represented Jehovah's presence, Zion was referred to as the place of God's dwelling and a place from which strength, blessing and salvation would come. (Psalms 20:2; 134:3; *14:7*)

Zion	Chapter X

    Zion is also referred to as the heavenly Jerusalem. In *Hebrews 12:22* it says, *"But ye are come unto mount Sion and unto the city of the living God, the heavenly Jerusalem, and to an innumerable company of angels."* We are citizens of a heavenly kingdom with so many angels that they are too numerous to be counted. Because the earthly Jerusalem was the capital city of Israel, the location of God's presence, the New Jerusalem will be the heavenly capital city where Jesus Christ will dwell and reign. (*Revelation 21:22*)

    The New Jerusalem is described as descending out of heaven from God and having the glory of God. The light that comes from the great city is like a jasper stone, clear as crystal. The city has walls that are 200 feet thick and 1400 miles high with twelve gates. Each gate has the name of one of the tribes of Israel on it. The city is laid out as a square where the length, height and width are each 1400 miles. The wall is of jasper and the city is pure gold, like clear glass. The foundations of the wall of the city are adorned with all kinds of precious stones having twelve layers. The first layer is made of jasper, the second sapphire, the third chalcedony, the fourth emerald, the fifth sardonyx, the sixth sardius, the seventh chrysolite, the eighth beryl, the ninth topaz, the tenth chrysoprase, the eleventh jacinth and the twelfth amethyst. Because of God's glory, there is no need for the sun or the moon to shine. The only people who will enter are those who are written in the Lamb's Book of Life. (*Revelation 21:9-23*)

The Message

When I sing, *"Zion"* I hear relationship. Relationship is "a state of connectedness." It is "a connection by blood or marriage." We as Christians are connected to Jesus because of the blood of the lamb. When we confessed with our mouth and believed in our heart that God raised Jesus Christ from the dead, a new relationship was initiated between Jesus Christ and His people. Our lives and our whole way of thinking changed. Our destiny changed. The things that we used to do and say were no longer desirable to us because there was a conviction on the inside of us. The Holy Spirit was leading and guiding us. The bible says, that when the Word of God falls on good ground, there was fruit and some had thirty, some had sixty and some had a hundred fold return. (*Mark 4:8*) Why did some have more than others? Because of relationship.

My relationship with my husband is not the same relationship it was when we were married over twelve years ago. Nor are we the same people. Over time, I grew to know him in an intimate way that no one else knows. I learned his likes and dislikes, what makes him happy, what makes him sad, I learned his body language and how he is feeling based on certain gestures. I learned how his day is going from the tones in his voice. I know my husband on a deeper level than anyone else. That is all because of relationship; from spending time with him, living with him, talking to him and loving him. I know him in a way that no one else will ever know. The more we grew to know one another, the more fruit we produced.

God wants the same from us. He wants a relationship with us. It has to go farther than just saying that we are saved. We should not be the same people or be on the same level with God that we were when we first believed. He wants us to grow together over time and know Him in an intimate way that no one else knows. He wants us to learn His likes and dislikes, what makes Him happy and what makes Him sad, to learn His body language and how He is feeling based on His gestures. To learn how His day is going from the tones in His voice. He wants us to know him on a deeper level than anyone else. In order for that to happen, we have to spend time with Him, live in Him, talk to Him and love Him. When that happens, then we produce fruit. Is it not what life is about? Being fruitful and glorifying God.

How do we glorify God? The first step is to confess with our mouth and believe in our heart that God raised His Son, Jesus Christ from the dead. (*Romans 10:9*) In the beginning when God created Adam and Eve, He told them that they could eat of any tree in the Garden of Eden except for the tree of knowledge of good and evil. Adam and Eve disobeyed God and ate of the tree. As a result, they were removed from the presence of God. They could no longer have a personal relationship with the Father. This displeased God because He created

Adam and Eve in His image and after His likeness to have dominion on the earth. When His presence was removed, they no longer reflected God and therefore, they no longer glorified Him.

When David took Zion from the Jebusites, He went to the house of Abinadab in Baale Judah, to get the Ark of God and bring to Zion. David understood the importance of the presence of God. The bible says that David and all the house of Israel played music before the Lord on all kinds of instruments. But when they came to Nachon's threshing floor, which is a floor or area on which grain is beaten out, the oxen stumbled. Uzzah, a son of Abinadab put his hand out to protect the ark and God was angry and killed him. (*2 Samuel 6:1-7*) Is it not wonderful to know that we do not have to work to get into the presence of God? All we had to do was confess and believe and we were in the presence of God.

As a result of Uzzah's death, David became afraid of the Lord and took the Ark to the house of Obed-Edom the Gittite. Even though we do not have to praise our way into the presence of God, we have to respect the presence of God and handle His presence with care. How do we respect the presence of God? We get to know Him so that we will know how to carry His presence. How do we get to know Him? We spend time with Him, live in Him, talk to Him and love Him.

To spend time with God means to spend time in His word *John 1:1* says, "*... the Word was with God and the Word was God.*" Reading his word is spending time with God. The more time you spend in the Word of God, the more you will know and understand God. Like the Psalmist said, my delight is in the Word, yet will I meditate day and night. (*Psalms 1:*2)

We must live in God. If we abide in Him and He abides in us, we can ask for what ever we choose, and it will be given. (*John 15:5*) To abide means "to dwell." When David took the Ark to the house of Obed-Edom, he left the Ark for three months and all of Obed-Edom's house was blessed.

We must talk to God. To talk means "to convey one's thoughts." Whether it be by your spoken words, hands, or writings, talking is how you know someone's thoughts. God will in turn convey His thoughts to us. When we have the mind of Christ, (*1 Corinthians 2:*16) then our thoughts become his thoughts.

We must love Him. When we initially accept Christ as our Savior, we may have Agape love for God but as we grow to know and understand Him, our Agape love will grow into Philia love. In other words, when we accept Jesus Christ as our personal Lord and Savior, we were exercising Agape love. A love that is governed by the principle or basic truth established by God. It may or may not have been accompanied by warmth or affection. But as we spent time with Him and learned of Him, and realized all the wonderful and marvelous things that He has done for us, we began to experience Philia love. A love of affection or a tender feeling that indicates personal attachment, as

THE MOTIVATION, MESSAGE AND MEANING BEHIND THE MUSIC

a matter of sentiment or feeling. In *Matthew 5:44*, God tells us to Agape love our enemies. We are to love them because the Word of God commands us to. This love does not mean that we necessarily have a personal relationship with them. I have Philia love for my husband and my children. I have deep warmth and affection for them.

This is also the difference between someone who praises God and someone is worships God. The bible says, *"Let everything that hath breath praise the Lord."* (*Psalms 150:6*) Anything living that breathes will praise the Lord but everyone that breathes can not worship Him. Why? Because it is all about relationship. We who worship Him, have taken the time to know Jesus on an intimate level so much so, we live, breath, eat and sleep, Jesus. Jesus becomes our lifestyle. Because we "live together" and talk to one another and spend time together, worship becomes our lifestyle. We become worship. We become Philia love.

When David was told how blessed Obed-Edom was as a result of the Ark being in his house, David went and brought up the Ark of God from the house of Obed-Edom to Zion. (*2 Samuel 6:12*) There are benefits to living in the presence of God. *Psalms 103:2* says, *"Bless the Lord, O my soul, and forget not all his benefits."* And *Psalms 116:12* says, *"What shall I render unto the Lord for all his benefits toward me?"* What are some of the benefits?

- You are blessed! To be blessed means that you have divine favor. You are blessed in the city, blessed in the country, blessed when you come in and blessed when you go out. You are the head and not the tail, you are above only and not beneath! (*Deuteronomy 28:3, 6, 13*)

- You have protection! *"No weapon formed against thee shall prosper; and every tongue that shall rise against thee in judgment thou shall condemn. This is the heritage of the servants of the Lord, and their righteousness is of me, saith the Lord."* (*Isaiah 54:17*)

- You are prosperous! *"This book of the law shall not depart out of thy mouth; but thou shalt meditate therein day and night, that thou mayest observe to do according to all that is written therein: for then thou shalt make thy way prosperous, and then thou shalt have good success."* (*Joshua 1:8*)

- You are never alone! *"...I will be with thee: I will not fail thee, nor forsake thee."* (*Joshua 1:5*)

- You are loved! *"For God so loved the world, that he gave his only begotten Son, that whosoever believeth in him should not perish but have everlasting life.* (*John 3:16*) There is no greater love than the love of a man who has laid his life down for you. (*John 15:13*)

- You have a friend! *"Ye are my friends...but I have called you friends; for all things that I* have heard of my Father I have made known unto you." (*John 15:14-15*)

- You have eternal life! Eternal means "being without end; existing outside of time." *"And this is the record, that God hath given to us eternal life, and this life is in his Son."* (*1 John 5:11*)

- Your name is written in the Lamb's book of life! Those names who are in the Lamb's book of life will enter into the New Jerusalem. (*Revelation 21:27*)

    Another way we glorify God is by being fruitful. When God created Adam and Eve, He told them to be fruitful and multiply. (*Genesis 1:28*) By doing so, the earth would be filled with images of God, therefore glorifying God. How can we be fruitful? *Galatians 5:22-23* says, *"But the fruit of the Spirit is love, joy, peace, longsuffering, gentleness, goodness, faith, meekness, temperance: against such there is no law."* As we grow in each of these areas, we will reflect more of the character of God and therefore produce fruit and glorify God.

- Love. One day when the Pharisees and Sadducees who were the religious leaders, were testing Jesus, they asked Jesus, *"Teacher, which is the great commandment in the law?"* Jesus answered, *"You shalt love the Lord thy God with all thy heart, and with all thy soul, and with all thy mind. This is the first and great* commandment. *And the second is like unto it, Thou shalt love thy neighbor as thyself.*" (*Matthew 22:34-39*) Jesus said that loving Him was the greatest commandment because if we truly love Him then we will naturally keep the commandments. As our relationship with God grows, our love for God should grow from Agape love to Philia love.

- Joy. To have joy means to have "intense and especially ecstatic or exultant happiness." If God dwells in us and we dwell in Him or His presence where there is fullness of joy and at his right-hand, pleasures forever more, then the more of His presence that we experience, the more joy we will have. (*Psalms 16:11*) In *Nehemiah 8:10* it says, "...*for the joy of the Lord is your strength.*" As we experience God's joy, we will grow stronger and in return please God and give Him greater joy.

- Peace. To have peace means to have "inner contentment." Jesus said, "*Peace I leave with you, my peace I give unto you: not as the world giveth, give I unto you. Let not your heart be troubled, neither let it be afraid.*" (*John 14:27*) If we have the peace of God, then nothing should be able to move us. We should have confident assurance in any conflict. So when tribulation comes in our life, we should be of good cheer because we have the peace of Christ. (*John 16:33*)

- Long-suffering. To have longsuffering means to have "patient endurance of pain or unhappiness." When God promised Abraham a son, Abraham patiently endured 25 years until Isaac was born. In *Hebrews 6:15* it says that Abraham patiently endured and he obtained the promise. If we patiently endure, we will receive that which God has promised us.

- Gentleness. To have gentleness means to have "mildness." In *2 Timothy 2:24* it says, *"And the servant of the Lord must not strive; but be gentle..."* In other words, we must not quarrel with man but if we are gentle, they will more than likely listen to what we have to say.

- Goodness. To have goodness means to have "kindness." *Romans 11:22* says, *"Behold therefore the goodness and severity of God: on them which fell, severity; but toward thee, goodness, if thou continue in his goodness: otherwise thou also shalt be cut off."* In other words, we are to exhibit the same kindness that Christ displayed. If we do not, then we will be cut off from the blessings of God.

- Faith. To have faith means to have "complete confidence." *"Now faith is the substance of things hoped for, the evidence of things not seen."* (*Hebrews 11:1*) If God has promised something to us, we are to wait with complete confidence even when we do not see the manifestation, and know that all the promises of God in Him are yes and in Him Amen, for the glory of God. (*2 Corinthians 1:20*)

- Meekness. To have meekness means to have "humility." *Titus 3:2* says, *"To speak evil of no man, to be no brawlers, but gentle, shewing all meekness unto all men."* The power of life and death are in the tongue and we have to watch what we say. We should speak life and not death even to those who wish to harm us. When we do speak to them, it should be done in humility.

- Temperance. To have temperance means to have "moderation and self-restraint, as in behavior or expression." *"Let your moderation be known unto all men."* (*Philippians 4:5*) We are to have self-restraint with people inside and outside of the church. We should not seek revenge against those who treat us unfairly.

I pray that you have enjoyed hearing my personal story as I share in great detail the motivation, message and meaning behind the songs that God has blessed me with.

In Chapter I, I stated that I was excited about researching the scriptures for myself because I know that by the time this book is completed, I will have grown spiritually and closer to God. Well I have! My relationship with God has blossomed like the rose of Sharon! When I arise in the morning,

THE MOTIVATION, MESSAGE AND MEANING BEHIND THE MUSIC

God is the first person on my mind and I immediately get down on my knees to pray. I don't get the kids off to school first or fix Benjamin's oatmeal first, but I thank God for His many blessings. I then put the instrumental portion of my CD on and I worship God. I worship in the afternoon and I worship in the evening. For the entire day, my thoughts are consumed with God and His goodness.

I absolutely love the place that I am in right now. I am so in love with Jesus that no matter what happens in my life, all is well with my soul. My outlook at life is different and refreshing. The things that I was so concerned about are no longer an issue. There is a peace within me that is unexplainable.

I continue to hear God's voice with great clarity and as a result I joined my church choir, "Sounds of Glory", I attend prayer on Friday evenings at my church and I partnered with my father to begin our own network consulting firm, "WIN Solutions." I thank God for my father and I can already see a book coming as a result of this partnership for fathers and daughters!

I pray that as a result of reading this book, the dreams that God has placed within you, come forth now, "in the name of Jesus." May you listen to the still small voice as the Holy Spirit gives you great clarity on how to pursue those dreams. God gave you those dreams that He may be glorified in the earth.

Now unto Him that is able to keep you from falling, and to present you faultless before the presence of His glory with exceeding joy. To the only wise God our Savior, be glory and majesty, dominion and power, both now and forever. Amen.

THE MOTIVATION, MESSAGE AND MEANING BEHIND THE MUSIC

About The Author

Maranda Marie Forney was born in Camden, New Jersey, January 2, 1969, to George and Charm Watkins. At the age of eight, Maranda and her family relocated to Chicago, Illinois. As a child she studied voice and piano for eight years winning several vocal competitions. During the summer of 1985, Maranda participated in the junior arts program at The University of Illinois, Urbana-Champaign campus. That same summer, Maranda and her family moved to Columbus, Ohio and for a brief moment, she was a member of a teen recording group for a major secular recording label. Spring of 1987 Maranda won the title of "Miss Alla Baba", 1st runner-up "Miss Cupidette", and was introduced into society as a Victory Matron Debutante.

In May of 1990 Maranda met her husband, Michael Calvin Forney working as a review examiner for an insurance company headquartered in Columbus, Ohio. In September of the following year, they both received Jesus Christ as their personal Lord and Savior under the ministry of Bishop Brian Keith and Prophetess Donna Williams and were married two weeks later. While a member of All Nations Church, Maranda participated on the Praise & Worship team, ANC Choir and performed several special selections.

After the birth of her second child in 1991, she decided to return to school. While working during the day, Maranda attended evening classes at DeVry Institute of Technology in Columbus, Ohio. In 1998, four children later, she received her Bachelors of Science in Electronic Engineering.

Post graduation, Maranda accepted a position with a global telecommunications company in Naperville, Illinois. In the Spring of 2001, Maranda and Michael had their fifth child, summer of 2002 their sixth child and fall of 2003 their seventh child.

Maranda and Michael Forney currently reside in the Chicago, Illinois area where they are members of Life Changers International Church, with Pastors Gregory and Grace Dickow. Maranda is a member of the "Sounds of Glory" choir where Pastor Keith Cistrunk is the head musician and pastor of the Life Changers International Church music department.

Maranda's background vocals can be heard on several projects including, "Without Faith I'm Nothing" by Rossi Howard and "Loose Control" by Tom Bynum. Maranda has written numerous songs and recorded her first project, "In Your Presence," in November of 2001. She is currently working on her second project, "Maranda Forney".

Maranda's motto and favorite scripture, "*I can do all things through Christ which strengtheneth me*," Philippians 4:13, has empowered her to be all that God has called her to be. The wife of Michael Calvin Forney, mother of seven beautiful children (Charm, Tatianna, Michael, Timothy, Benjamin, Joseph and Amirah),

THE MOTIVATION, MESSAGE AND MEANING BEHIND THE MUSIC

Worshipper, Psalmist, Songwriter, Entrepreneur (established MNet Services in the Spring of 1999, Forney Publishing, a BMI affiliate in the Summer of 2001 and WIN Solutions February of 2004) and a Servant of God.

You may contact Maranda the following ways:

Mailing Address
Maranda Forney
P.O. Box 806394
Chicago, Illinois 60680-6394

Telephone
(847) 687-7811

Email
mforney@marandaonline.com

Website
http://www.marandaonline.com

Endnotes

[i] *Merriam-Webster's Collegiate Dictionary Tenth Edition.* Springfield, Massachusetts: Merriam-Webster, Incorporated, 1993.

[ii] *Insight On The Scriptures Volume I: Aaron-Jehoshua.* Brooklyn, New York: Watch Tower Bible And Tract Society Of Pennsylvania International Bible Students Association, 1988.

[iii] Miller, Madeleine S. and Miller, J. Lane, *Harper's Bible Dictionary.* New York, New York: Harper & Brothers, 1954.

[iv] *Insight On The Scriptures Volume I: Jehovah-Zuzim.* Brooklyn, New York: Watch Tower Bible And Tract Society Of Pennsylvania International Bible Students Association, 1988.